KU-259-788

Lea

Baile Át
Dublin

BASKETBALL NOW!

ADAM ELLIOTT SEGAL

BASKETBALL NOW!

THE STARS AND STORIES OF THE NBA

FIREFLY BOOKS

A FIREFLY BOOK

Published by Firefly Books Ltd. 2015

Copyright © 2015 Firefly Books Ltd.
Text copyright © Adam Elliott Segal
Images copyright as listed on page 159

All rights reserved. No part of this publication may be reproduced, stored in a retrieval system, or transmitted in any form or by any means, electronic, mechanical, photocopying, recording or otherwise, without the prior written permission of the Publisher or a license from The Canadian Copyright Licensing Agency (Access Copyright). For an Access Copyright license, visit www. accesscopyright.ca or call toll free to 1-800-893-5777.

First printing

Publisher Cataloging-in-Publication Data (U.S.)
Segal, Adam Elliott.
Basketball now! : the stars and stories of the National Basketball Association / Adam Elliott Segal.
[160] pages : color photographs ; cm.
Includes index.
Summary: Profiles of 50 profiles on the best players in the National Basketball Association include action shots in color.
ISBN-13: 978-1-77085-576-2 (pbk.)
1. National Basketball Association -- Biography. 2. National Basketball Association – Pictorial works. 3. Basketball – Biography. 4. Basketball – Pictorial works. I. Title.
796.323/0922 dc23   GV884.A1.S443 2015

Library and Archives Canada Cataloguing in Publication
Segal, Adam Elliott, author
Basketball now! : the stars and stories of the NBA / Adam Elliott Segal.
Includes index.
ISBN 978-1-77085-576-2 (paperback)
1. Basketball players--United States--Biography. 2. National Basketball Association--Biography. 3. Basketball players--United States. 4. Basketball--United States--History. I. Title.
 GV884.A1S44 2015   796.323'640922   C2015-904119-8

Published in the United States by
Firefly Books (U.S.) Inc.
P.O. Box 1338, Ellicott Station
Buffalo, New York 14205

Published in Canada in 2015 by
Firefly Books Ltd.
50 Staples Avenue, Unit 1
Richmond Hill, Ontario L4B 0A7

Cover and interior design: Matt Filion

Printed in Canada

The publisher gratefully acknowledges the financial support for our publishing program by the Government of Canada through the Canada Book Fund as administered by the Department of Canadian Heritage.

CONTENTS

INTRODUCTION

THE 2014-15 NBA season was a banner year. From start to finish, the 82-game schedule showcased competitive, nonstop action and was one of the more intriguing seasons in recent memory. In many ways it's felt like a changing of the guard. Coming off four straight appearances in the NBA Finals by the Miami Heat and the fifth championship for the San Antonio Spurs in 2014, it was refreshing to see the emergence of the Golden State Warriors, Memphis Grizzlies and Atlanta Hawks. But it wasn't all new—LeBron James returned to Cleveland this season and hoisted a motley crew of castoffs all the way to Game 6 of the Finals, posting numbers along the way that are simply unheard of in the modern era. With several aging superstars on the shelf for most of the year—Kobe Bryant, Carmelo Anthony—a new class of rising stars began to shine, players like DeMarcus Cousins, Kyle Lowry, Klay Thompson and Russell Westbrook. Rookies arrived in full force—number one overall Andrews Wiggins proved he deserved the tag as future of the franchise despite a tough first season in the win–loss column. Alongside fellow rookie and Slam Dunk Contest winner Zach LaVine, Wiggins looks to change the fortunes in Minnesota.

LaVine's performance at the aforementioned dunk contest was a throwback and a revelation, so it felt like perfect timing to include an essay on the history of the dunk contest. As I spoke to basketball fans of all ages throughout the season, countless smiles emerged when I asked them to recount their favorite dunk contest moments (Vince Carter by a landslide) or the posters on their walls of Dominique Wilkins or Dee Brown flying through the air. LaVine's off-the-charts slams at the 2015 Slam Dunk Contest should provide the same fodder for a younger generation of basketball fans.

If, like me, you tuned in to watch the Golden State Warriors because of the magic that Steph Curry spun all season, you watched one of the truly unique talents in recent memory. It felt like we were witnessing in real time the birth of an NBA superstar, and the newly crowned MVP, alongside fellow Splash Brother Klay Thompson, led the Warriors all the way to a finals win over the Cleveland Cavaliers. The torch has clearly been passed to a slender, lights-out shooter with dribbling skills reminiscent of John Stockton or Allen Iverson. The Warriors are part of a new NBA.

Storied franchises such as the Lakers and Knicks were predictably awful as both franchises began rebuilding. Tim Duncan, he of five rings with the San Antonio Spurs, could have gracefully exited the game after nearly two decades of service, but he's coming back for one more kick at the crown. The triangle offense so popular a decade ago is nearly extinct. A new style is taking over, with players like Curry leading the way. It's a guard-heavy game, with a premium being put on three-point shooting, especially in transition, and from a management side on analytics, finding diamonds in the rough late in the draft and turning them into stars, all for half the price of a lottery pick.

In the early 90s, during the golden years of the Chicago Bulls' first three-peat, my two best friends and I spent every hour we could playing 21 in my alleyway. I thought a lot about those days while writing this book: those lazy summer days shooting hoops, that mini Bulls ball I kept in my room, pretending to be Jordan hitting a game-winning shot. I thought about all the Toronto Raptors fans I met this season while watching my local team, young and old, from all backgrounds, and how exciting it's been to watch hoops in an emerging market that's thrown off the shackles of ineptitude, trading it for a bright future (just be careful not to mention Paul Pierce around these parts). It must be a similar feeling in places like Milwaukee, Minnesota and Orlando, rabid fan bases that just want a chance to taste playoff success. It appears they will soon enough.

It feels like the NBA is changing, growing, moving toward an exciting future, thanks to players like James Harden, Anthony Davis, Kevin Durant and a host of others. Although we couldn't include every rising star or next rookie phenom, we hope there's something for everyone in this book, whether it's the current crop of superstars, rising stars, top international players, unsung heroes or next set of rookies to emerge into the limelight. Stats and analytics may be creeping into the mainstream consciousness, but I hope that, like me, you remember why you fell in love with basketball in the first place: series-ending buzzer beaters, unforgettable dunks, dominant 50-point performances out of nowhere. And although we may agree to disagree on who is the greatest player of all time, or the gnarliest dunker, or the most clutch playoff performer or the worst draft pick in NBA history, I know we can agree on one thing: we love this game.

LeBron James drives hard to the rim against Tony Snell of the Chicago Bulls in 2015. James helped the Cavaliers franchise get some measure of revenge against long-standing rival Chicago, by defeating them in the second round of the 2015 playoffs.

Dublin City Public Libraries

CARMELO ANTHONY 12 / KOBE BRYANT 14 / STEPHEN CURRY 16 / TIM DUNCAN 18
KEVIN DURANT 20 / BLAKE GRIFFIN 22 / JAMES HARDEN 24 / LEBRON JAMES 26
CHRIS PAUL 28 / DERRICK ROSE 30 / DWYANE WADE 32 / RUSSELL WESTBROOK 34

STEPHEN CURRY

CARMELO ANTHONY 7

IT MAY SEEM early to call Carmelo Anthony one of the best ballers the world has ever seen, but consider this—just three games into the 2014–15 season, Anthony became the 40th player to ever reach the 20,000-point plateau, the sixth youngest to do so.

Twelve years in the NBA and it feels like Anthony's always been an offensive juggernaut in the league. But the New York native was once a gangly teen at Towson Catholic High School in Maryland and Oak Hill Academy in Virginia before setting his sights on Syracuse University, where he led the Orangemen as a freshman to a national title in 2003. He dropped 33 against Texas in the Final Four and went 20 and 10 versus Kansas in the deciding game.

In one of the deepest drafts in recent memory, 'Melo went third overall in 2003 behind the consensus number one LeBron James and the soon-to-be-forgotten Darko Milicic. Anthony led the Denver Nuggets to six straight playoff appearances but rarely farther than the first round.

He made an immediate impact his first season, taking the 17-65 Nuggets the year before he arrived to 43-39, good for eighth in the West. Despite the success, the Nuggets were ousted in five games by Minnesota, and Anthony would finish second in Rookie of the Year voting to King James. But his strong rookie season—21 points per game, 6 rebounds and 3 assists—was impressive nonetheless.

A slow and steady rise up the NBA's career scoring ladder has been a testament to Anthony's talent and willingness to work hard. By his third year, he was averaging 26.5 points per game. He torched the 76ers in that 2005–06 season for 45 points and developed a reputation for hitting clutch game-winning shots. Despite finishing third in the conference, the Nuggets bowed out to the Clippers in the playoffs, and owing to his most successful season to that point, the Nuggets signed Anthony to a five-year, $80 million deal.

At 6-foot-8 and 240 pounds, he was no longer a gangly teenager who skipped class and didn't pay attention to detail. He became an All-Star and remained one for four of those five seasons, although he finished the fifth season as a New York Knick after a trade partway through 2010–11.

Anthony led the NBA in scoring in 2012–13 on a poor Knicks squad, but what most fans will remember is the colossal 62-point affair at Madison Square Garden on January 24, 2014. That night the ball acted like it was on a string attached to 'Melo's hands. He set two records that evening: most points by a Knick (previously 60, set in 1984 by Bernard King) and most points ever scored by an individual in MSG (previously held by Kobe Bryant's 61 in 2009). And Anthony didn't even play the final 7:18 of the game that night versus the Charlotte Hornets. He finished 23 for 25, 6 of 11 from beyond the three-point line and 10 of 10 from the free throw line, and he even added 13 rebounds, etching himself in the pantheon of greatest performances in basketball history.

"I was just locked in," he said following the contest. "The focus that I had, I felt like it was going to be a good night. There's only a small group of people that knows what that zone feels like." Perhaps even more impressive—he took the second fewest free throws among the 30 60-point games logged since the 1963–64 season.

As Anthony continues his march on the record book, his legend grows—currently he is approaching 30th all-time in points scored. He's represented his team at the All-Star Game seven times and twice won gold at the Olympics. But all this won't matter in the ring-crazy NBA if Anthony can't take a team deep into the playoffs, something that has eluded him since his days at Syracuse. The Knicks are still a work in progress on the way to becoming a true contender, and Anthony's dealing

with chronic back and knee problems that saw him miss a sizable portion of 2014–15. But with Phil Jackson and his 13 rings attempting to turn around the Knicks organization, Anthony has committed to staying in his hometown for the foreseeable future. If he stays healthy, will he go down as this generation's Patrick Ewing—the best Knick to never win a title? Or will he be the one to finally deliver New York their first championship since 1973?

CAREER HIGHLIGHTS

- Named an NBA All-Rookie (First Team) in 2003–04
- Has played in eight NBA All-Star Games (2007, 2008, 2010–2015)
- Won an Olympic gold medal with the U.S. men's basketball team in Beijing in 2008 and London in 2012
- Was the NBA scoring champion in 2012–13
- Set a career high in points (62) in 2013–14

LOS ANGELES LAKERS

POSITION SHOOTING GUARD / **SHOOTS** RIGHT / **HEIGHT** 6'6" / **WEIGHT** 212 LB. / **DRAFTED** 1996, CHARLOTTE HORNETS, 13TH OVERALL

KOBE BRYANT 24

JUMPING FROM HIGH school to the National Basketball Association isn't for everyone. Then again, everyone isn't Kobe Bryant. Over his storied career—from high-school phenom to NBA royalty—he has etched his name among the ranks of the league's true great superstars and consummate winners.

Born in Philadelphia to a basketball-playing father, Joe "Jellybean" Bryant, Kobe was raised in Italy before returning to the United States after his father's playing career. He was the best high school player in the country in the mid-1990s, leading Lower Merion High to its first state championship in over 50 years, averaging more than 30 points per game. Bryant was drafted 13th overall by the Charlotte Hornets in 1996, and his rights were traded to the Los Angeles Lakers for Vlade Divac. He's been a Laker ever since.

But the NBA great wasn't an immediate superstar his first few years in California. He averaged just over 15 minutes per game backing up Nick Van Exel in 1996–97, putting up a pedestrian 7.6 points per contest during his rookie season. But at just 18 years of age, he won the 1997 Slam Dunk Contest, just one year removed from taking pop star Brandy to the prom. Bryant, with no shortage of swagger, had announced his arrival on the big stage, propelling himself down the road to stardom.

Although his third year in the NBA was marred by a labor strike, Bryant's

playing time increased, as did his numbers that season—19.9 points per game, 84 percent from the free-throw line, 5.3 rebounds and 3.8 assists. The following year, however, changed the course of his career forever, or more aptly, one man altered Bryant's destiny.

The arrival of Phil Jackson in the 1999–2000 season was no small coup for the Lakers organization, and Bryant flourished under the new head coach, the architect of six championships with the Chicago Bulls. Jackson's triangle offense, so successful in the Windy City, had the same effect in LA, and the team won 67 games under the tutelage of the master. The size and freakish athleticism of center Shaquille O'Neal in the paint freed up Kobe, and his per-game

point totals rose dramatically, from 19.9 before Jackson to 22.5 in year 1 and 28.5 in year 2. Kobe and Shaq would three-peat as champions, but behind the scenes, the foundation and friendship between the two stars was cracking. The feud led to O'Neal's being traded to Miami following the Lakers' loss to Detroit in the 2004 finals. But perhaps without Shaq's departure, basketball fans would have never seen one of the greatest single performances of all-time.

January 22, 2006, will go down as a night to remember. Some forget that the Lakers were losing to the Toronto Raptors by 18 at one point, and it set Kobe off on a scoring tear. He shot 28 of 46 that night, 7 of 13 from beyond the arc, and hit a remarkable 18 of 20 free throws. He scored 28 of the Lakers' 31 points in the fourth quarter en route to an 81-point performance. He accounted for 66 percent of his team's 122 points and somehow found the time to bring down 6 boards and dish out 2 assists. Coach Jackson, he of 13 championship rings, said of Kobe's dominance that night, "I've seen some remarkable games, but I've never seen one like that before." It is the second highest total scored by any player

in NBA history, placing Bryant behind only Wilt Chamberlain's 100-point game in 1962. And if you've ever wondered what fueled such a mind-blowing performance, it was simple: pepperoni pizza.

But Bryant's critics wouldn't abate. According to them, it was Shaq who had made Kobe a champion, and all the scoring feats in the world couldn't erase that point. So Bryant set out to shut down his critics. He won the league MVP in 2008, getting 82 percent of the first-place votes, and then led his Lakers to back-to-back rings in 2009 and 2010. Those two titles made him a five-time champion, putting him in conversation with other greats like Michael Jordan and Magic Johnson. Kobe was named finals MVP both times, and it was clear his legacy had far surpassed O'Neal's with his postseason heroics.

Entering his 19th season in 2014–15, Bryant was coming off recurring injuries but appeared to be healthy before tearing his rotator cuff dunking the ball in late January. An elusive sixth ring now feels unlikely for the former MVP. The Lakers are undeniably still his team, despite the fact they're in rebuild mode.

CAREER HIGHLIGHTS

- Named NBA Most Valuable Player for 2007–08
- Named MVP of the NBA Finals twice (2008–09, 2009–10)
- Won an Olympic gold medal with the U.S. men's basketball team in Beijing in 2008 and London in 2012
- Led the NBA in points for four seasons (2002–03 and 2005–06 to 2007–08)
- Averaged a career-high 35.4 points per game in 2005–06, which is the eighth highest average in NBA history

His career numbers make him a lock for the Hall of Fame—25.4 points per game, 5.3 rebounds, 4.8 assists, 33 percent three-point shooting, 84 percent from the free-throw line. And during the Lakers' dismal season, Kobe passed Jordan on the all-time points list and now sits third, scoring his 32,293rd point on a free throw. Bryant said after the game it was a "huge honor."

The honor's been all ours.

POSITION POINT GUARD / **SHOOTS** RIGHT / **HEIGHT** 6'3" / **WEIGHT** 190 LB. / **DRAFTED** 2009, GOLDEN STATE WARRIORS, 7TH OVERALL

STEPHEN CURRY 30

HIS SHOT IS as pure as they come: a sweet stroke that finds nothing but net from whatever corner of the earth he hoists it. Stephen Curry was born to shoot basketballs. Whether it be a full-speed breakout-to-pull-up three or a slash to the hoop, he's graceful and almost effortless. Mostly, Steph Curry is a star.

Born Wardell Stephen Curry II in 1990, the point guard comes from basketball pedigree, the son of former NBA player Dell Curry. He spent 16 years in the league and finished his career with the Toronto Raptors, a city where his oldest son Steph spent formidable time playing 1-on-1 in shootarounds with Vince Carter and Tracy McGrady before his undeniable talent led him to star in high school in Charlotte, North Carolina, where Dell now works as an analyst for the Hornets. Despite impressive numbers, Curry was overlooked by major schools, so he took his trade to Davidson College, one of the smallest schools in the NCAA I division.

His arrival put the school on the map, and in Curry's first appearance in the NCAA tournament, he dropped 30 points in a loss to fourth-seeded Maryland.

The following year, Curry put 40 on the board against seventh-seeded Gonzaga, the first tourney win for Davidson since 1969. The Wildcats then rattled off victories against second-seeded Georgetown and third-seeded Wisconsin before bowing out to the eventual champion, Kansas.

Davidson's magical run was over, but Curry had emerged as one to watch. He averaged 28.6 points per game his final year of college before entering the 2009 NBA Draft, where he was selected seventh overall by the Golden State Warriors. Since then, he's amazed with his skill. He finished second in Rookie of the Year voting in 2009–10 and second in the NBA in steals while recording his first triple-double (36 points, 13 assists, 10 rebounds). He punctuated his first season by putting up 42 points, 9 boards and 8 assists against Portland in the final game of the season.

Listed at 6-foot-3, Curry's simply become the most dynamic point guard in the game. He already holds the top two spots in the NBA record books for most threes made in one season (286, 2014–15; 272, 2012–13) and sports a career 44 percent mark from downtown. He posted career-best numbers in 2013–14: 24.5 points per game, 8.5 assists, 4.3 rebounds. Despite the emergence of shooting guard Klay Thompson in 2014–15, Curry's numbers remained almost unchanged. He led the Warriors to the best record in the NBA and was named MVP for his all-round game and lights-out shooting.

There's something special about the way he does it all. Aside from the silky smooth release, his basketball IQ is through the roof. One minute he's running the floor off a steal and dunking with authority; the next he's settling the offense down and dishing no-lookers to a trailing teammate. His bag of tricks includes a killer crossover, spot-up three, circus shots that seem impossible and a behind-the-back pass that is difficult to intercept. He's also had his share of seemingly impossible to hit game-winning baskets. One announcer called him "a video-game player" last season after a spectacular sequence where he hit a three, then stole the inbounds pass and went up and under the hoop for another bucket. He seems to regularly blow up Twitter with his shimmy-shake fakes, and his ball-handling skills are reinventing the way the game is played.

Curry's nearly a career 90 percent free-throw shooter and goes more than 43 percent from three-point land. His highlight-reel season of 2014–15 included 30 points and 15 assists in a 136–115 shootout versus the Lakers in November; 8 of 11 threes for 40 points, 7 assists and 6 rebounds in a win versus Miami several weeks later; 34 points, 9 assists, 7 rebounds, 4 steals and 1 block against the Oklahoma Thunder; and an astronomical 10 from beyond the arc in February against Dallas, finishing with 51 points, the most he's ever scored on home court.

He destroyed the competition en route

CAREER HIGHLIGHTS

to an NBA Finals berth, taking down New Orleans, Memphis and Houston along the way. Curry was the straw that stirred the drink, hitting miraculous game-winning shots from the corner, dancing his way to the rim or dropping 30-plus with regularity—including 37 in Game 5 of the finals. The Warriors captured the 2015 NBA Championship, their first in 40 years, and Curry set a playoff record for most threes with 98.

The main question about the most creative player in the league, who demolished the NBA in 2014–15, is can anyone stop him?

- Named NBA Most Valuable Player for 2014–15
- Named an NBA All-Rookie (First Team) in 2009–10
- Named Rookie of the Month three times in 2009–10
- Set the NBA record for three-pointers in a single season (272) in 2012–13; broke his own record in 2014–15 with 286
- Active NBA leader in career three-point field goal percentage (.440)

SAN ANTONIO SPURS

POSITION POWER FORWARD–CENTER / **SHOOTS** RIGHT / **HEIGHT** 6'11" / **WEIGHT** 250 LB. / **DRAFTED** 1997, SAN ANTONIO SPURS, 1ST OVERALL

TIM DUNCAN 21

FEW MEN IN the game of basketball deserve the platitudes that have been heaped upon them. Tim Duncan is one of those players, and the superlatives know no bounds when describing one of the true class acts of the game. At the very least, the San Antonio Spurs center is entitled to call himself a legend, a one-franchise guy who became the foundation of a dynasty, and over the course of his career, set the bar for future generations to come.

With more than 1,500 games under his belt, Duncan's career is as storied as they come. Not flashy or gregarious, he simply went about his business, defining a modern-era standard of 20 points and 10 rebounds and harkening back to the old days of gentle big men plying their trade in the paint. His statistics stand for themselves, testaments to durability and a consistency difficult to keep up with age. His career per-game line is 19.5 points, 11 rebounds and a .500 shooting percentage. He has five NBA titles (alongside the likes of David Robinson, Manu Ginobili and Tony Parker) and is a two-time NBA MVP and a 15-time All-Star.

Duncan was a consensus number one in a bad draft. But before he jumped to the NBA, the Virgin Islands–born center attended Wake Forest University, where he spent four years honing his craft and bucking the trend to leave college early. A standout swimmer in his early teens, Duncan slowly graduated to basketball on the small island when a storm destroyed the swimming pool. He shifted to the hardcourt, and the rest is history. He's had only one coach in Gregg Popovich, who arrived midway through the 1996–97 season after an injury-riddled year for then-star player Robinson sent the Spurs spiraling to the basement, where they landed the lottery

CAREER HIGHLIGHTS

- Named NBA Most Valuable Player twice (2001–02, 2002–03)
- Named MVP of the NBA Finals three times (1998–99, 2002–03, 2004–05)
- Named NBA Rookie of the Year for 1997–98
- Has posted at least 10 rebounds per game in 13 of his 18 NBA seasons
- Has 2,942 blocks, which puts him sixth all-time in NBA history

1997–98 with All-Star numbers (21.1 points and 11.9 rebounds per game), establishing himself as one of the top centers offensively to go along with sturdy, reliable defensive play. In 1999, Duncan's second season and the year of the lockout, the Spurs started off poorly at 6-8. The fans were getting restless for change and Popovich's job was on the line, but in a pivotal game, Duncan dropped 23 points and 14 boards and added 5 blocks to defeat their cross-state rivals, the Houston Rockets. The Spurs lost just five more games all season, winning their first of five NBA titles with Pops at the helm and Duncan in the paint, adding three championships over the span of five years the following decade.

In 2001–02, Duncan posted a career high 25.5 points, adding 12.7 boards as he wrestled the mantle of franchise player from teammate Robinson. The following season, when the Spurs won their second title, Robinson's last, Duncan posted career highs in rebounds, assists and blocks—12.9 boards, 3.9 dimes and 2.9 stuffs, respectively. In his first six seasons in the league, he missed eight games, averaging nearly 39 minutes every year. He has been on a basketball court more than 55,000 minutes, including regular season and playoffs. It's almost a sheer wonder his body is still intact. In the 2003 playoffs, in 24 games, Duncan's 42.5 minutes per game on the court yielded almost unfathomable numbers—24.7 points, 15.4 boards, 5.3 assists, and more than 3 blocks per game en route to NBA Finals MVP.

He's a man you build around, what one former teammate called a "gym rat," with "a guard's passion for the game in a big body." He has an affinity for paintball, a fear of sharks and an indomitable work ethic masked under a mild-mannered attitude. But he's vicious on the court, competitive as they come, just not a typical NBA player who craves the spotlight 24/7. He's top 10 all-time in rebounding, top 15 in scoring and sixth in blocks (just behind Robinson). He's a surefire Hall of Famer and will long be remembered as one of the great players of the modern era.

pick in 1997 that became Duncan. One front office man once referred to Duncan and Popovich as "soul mates" when the Spurs marched toward another title in 2014, their fifth and likely their last together. They will certainly go down as one of the longest-serving and most successful duos of coach/player in sports history. Think Bill Belichick and Tom Brady in the NFL or Red Auerbach and Bill Russell in the old-school NBA.

Duncan won Rookie of the Year in

POSITION SMALL FORWARD–SHOOTING GUARD / **SHOOTS** RIGHT / **HEIGHT** 6'9" / **WEIGHT** 240 LB. / **DRAFTED** 2007, SEATTLE SUPERSONICS, 2ND OVERALL

KEVIN DURANT 35

PURE, UNADULTERATED TALENT. That's what you see when watching the 2014 MVP; it's like someone created Kevin Durant in a basketball laboratory. He oozes talent and flashes brilliance, all while maintaining a humble, low-key personality that's made him into one of the great heirs to the modern basketball throne.

Durant grew up in Seat Pleasant, on the outskirts of Washington, D.C., where his mother worked long shifts hauling 70-pound mailbags for the postal service while his grandmother and great aunt helped raise him. Gangly, he entered an elementary school gym and quickly learned the game under the supervision of a life-changing mentor nicknamed Chucky, who was shot to death when Durant was in high school. To honor his mentor, the future NBA superstar changed his number to 35, Chucky's age when he died. Chucky's death hardened the shy Durant, and he immersed himself in basketball. Durant was a quiet leader, a lethal shooter and someone unafraid to want the rock all the time. He wrote "Keep it Positive" on his massive shoes.

He played just one season at the University of Texas at Austin, averaging 25.8 points, and was drafted to the NBA second overall in 2007 behind major bust Greg Oden. Durant took his not going first overall as a slight.

The Seattle SuperSonics, who became the Oklahoma City Thunder in 2008, won only 20 games with their fresh draft choice in the backcourt in 2007–08, but he was skinny, he shot the ball too much, he had a poor diet and his game appeared one-dimensional. He was nicknamed "Starvin' Marvin."

By the time the team had moved to Oklahoma, everything changed. Durant was always in the gym, always shooting,

always leading by example. His coach, Scott Brooks, called him "good boring" and went on to say the only other man so young to lead a team the way Durant led the Thunder was Magic Johnson. Despite a 3-29 start, Oklahoma won 20 of their last 30, and change was in the air.

In 2009–10, Durant won the scoring title at 21 years of age, the youngest ever to do so. He continued dominating the league, leading Oklahoma to the Western Conference finals in 2011 and the NBA Finals the following season, falling 4-1 to the LeBron James–led Miami Heat. It's as close as he's been to tasting champagne.

Durant scorched the NBA for a career-high 32 points per game, 7.4 rebounds and 5.5 assists during his MVP season in 2013–14, punctuated by his heart-wrenching acceptance speech where he thanked his mom by saying, "You're the real MVP." He was a cool 87 percent from the line and 39 percent from deep. His 51-point game versus the Raptors was the stuff of legends. In 52 minutes on the floor, he was 7 of 12 from three-point land. He added 12 boards and 7 assists in a double OT thriller on the road, with Durant silencing the home crowd with 1.7 seconds left to play with a game-winning three, his second 50-plus game that year. The six-time All-Star

CAREER HIGHLIGHTS

- Named NBA Most Valuable Player for 2013–14
- Named NBA Rookie of the Year for 2007–08
- Named the All-Star Game MVP in 2011–12
- Won an Olympic gold medal with the U.S. men's basketball team in London in 2012
- Led the NBA in points for five consecutive seasons (2009–10 to 2013–2014)

finished the season with three triple-doubles in what may have been his finest campaign to date.

Durant lost much of the 2014–15 season to injury. He was diagnosed with a chronic foot problem in the summer after his MVP season and it never fully healed; he needed three separate surgeries to repair a fracture in his right foot. He played only 27 games and the Thunder missed the playoffs. Durant still managed 25.4 points per game while in the lineup, and the big positive from the lost season was the revelation of teammate Russell Westbrook. The point guard dominated the league in stretches that recalled Michael Jordan's fiefdom and finished as the league's scoring leader.

Next season may be the Thunder's last chance to go deep with their current roster—Durant's and Westbrook's contracts are up within a year of each other. If Durant opts for free agency in 2016—rumors continue to percolate that he will return to the D.C. area—the Thunder are well poised with the emergence of Westbrook as more superstar than sidekick if Durant does abdicate his post. He'll need to start winning championships to secure his legacy, and with LeBron dragging an injured Cavs team to the 2015 NBA Finals, his fifth in as many years, Durant's got a lot of catching up to do.

At 27 years old, the four-time scoring champion is the purest, most natural scorer in the NBA. No one doubts the talent. No one doubts the numbers. But until we see a ring, the jury's out on Durant. He may be a prince in waiting until the current king, LeBron James, decides to bestow him the crown.

LOS ANGELES CLIPPERS

POSITION POWER FORWARD / **SHOOTS** RIGHT / **HEIGHT** 6'10" / **WEIGHT** 250 LB. / **DRAFTED** 2009, LOS ANGELES CLIPPERS, 1ST OVERALL.

BLAKE GRIFFIN 32

BLAKE GRIFFIN LIKELY needs no introduction. You've probably seen him soaring through the air, high above the rim, waiting for a lob pass from teammate Chris Paul before slamming the ball into the bucket below. Griffin is more than just the meat and potatoes of the Los Angeles Clippers franchise—he's a multidimensional power forward who's quickly become one of the most versatile and exciting players in the NBA, a superstar since day one.

At 6-foot-10 and 250 pounds, it's hard to contend with his size. Griffin's a muscular, agile forward, with speed to the hoop and Superman-like ability to play above the rim. He was born in Oklahoma City and suited up for the Sooners in college. By his sophomore season, he'd emerged as the best player in the country; he declared for the draft after notching 22.7 points per game and 14.4 rebounds in his second year at Oklahoma.

Taken number one overall by the Clippers, Griffin's presence immediately changed the franchise—although it took an extra year for the transformation to happen on the floor, thanks to a preseason knee injury that kept him sidelined for all of 2009–10. By the time he finally threw on a Clips jersey, Griffin's star-like abilities were obvious. He twice topped 40 points in 2010–11, dropping 44 against New York early in the season and 47 versus Indiana later that campaign. He was a unanimous choice for Rookie of the Year, beating out

future All-Star John Wall and becoming the first rookie since Ralph Sampson in 1984 to sweep the award. He averaged 22.1 points, 12.1 boards and 3.8 assists. But

it wasn't just that. Griffin managed two triple-doubles and amassed a miraculous 63 double-doubles for the third highest total in the league. He finished three shy of

CAREER HIGHLIGHTS

- Named NBA Rookie of the Year for 2010–11
- Has played in five All-Star Games (2011–2015)
- Won the NBA Slam Dunk Contest in 2011
- Is a three-time All-NBA Second Team selection (2011–12, 2012–13, 2013–14)
- Has been in the top 10 for two-point field goals in all five seasons he has played (2010–11 to 2014–15)

fortunes would change when they traded for Paul later that year.

The pair immediately became the core of Lob City, a high-flying, acrobatic group that was a threat from the air every time they ran the ball upcourt during the lockout-shortened season of 2011–12. The Clips finished 40-26 and made the postseason for the first time since 2006, ringing in a new era in Los Angeles despite a second-round loss to the San Antonio Spurs. In their first full season together the following year, Paul and Griffin continued to wreak havoc. Despite a slight dip in his numbers, Griffin still led the team with averages of 18 points and 8.7 boards, while Paul dished out 9.7 dimes per game. The team finished 56-26 but fell to the Memphis Grizzlies in the first round, a disappointing exit for a strong team.

In 2014–15 the Clippers' longtime center DeAndre Jordan had a career year (he posted the second highest field goal percentage in NBA history), and despite an up-and-down season for the Clips that saw them score the second most points per game in the league while giving up the 16th most—all while still shaking off the cobwebs from the fallout of the Donald Sterling affair—the team still finished 56-26. Griffin suffered an elbow injury in early 2015 that kept him out of the lineup for 15 games, but he came back strong, torching the Golden State Warriors for 40 points and 12 rebounds in just his ninth game back.

Although his numbers may be slightly down—perhaps due to Jordan's emergence up the middle—Griffin has added to his game, unleashing a new step-back jumper that's nearly automatic when he's left open. It used to be that Griffin would almost always take the ball to the hoop. Now defenders need to do a little guesswork.

The Clippers will go only as far as their superstar power forward takes them. Diversifying his look is a good step forward for Griffin in appeasing the long-starved Clippers fans desperate for a title and bragging rights in a crowded California market.

that year's leader, Dwight Howard, a staggering achievement for a rookie.

Griffin's spectacular first year had shades of another great's rookie campaign. Shaquille O'Neal, the former LA Lakers and Orlando Magic star, posted 23.9 points and 13.9 rebounds his inaugural year in the league, and he added 3.5 blocks. Despite this, O'Neal was not a unanimous selection for best first-year player like Griffin. Upon receiving the award in 2011, Griffin said, "To miss my entire first year and then be able to be up here today is definitely satisfying." The Clippers, however, didn't make the playoffs, finishing 32-50. The team's

POSITION SHOOTING GUARD / **SHOOTS** LEFT / **HEIGHT** 6'5" / **WEIGHT** 225 LB. / **DRAFTED** 2009, OKLAHOMA CITY THUNDER, 3RD OVERALL

JAMES HARDEN 13

JAMES HARDEN IS hard to miss. He's more beard than ball, more flash than pan. Coming to the NBA via Arizona State as the third overall pick in 2009, Harden's become one of the league's true superstars, and perhaps the most unique one at that. Thanks to his myriad skills as well as his bushy, hard-to-miss chin, he's propelling the Houston Rockets to the top of the NBA class.

Harden was born in Bellflower, California, and he played ball at the same Los Angeles high school as former NBA players the O'Bannon brothers and Jason Kapono. A myth pervaded that Harden's first coach deemed him an NBA star upon first sight, but in 2012 he said simply that he could tell Harden "was going to be a good high school player." What's unmistakable is the shooting guard had gifts early on, and his Artesia High team won two state championships before he accepted a scholarship to Arizona State, following in the footsteps of his high school coach.

Taken third by the Oklahoma Thunder, Harden found himself outside the starting five on a stacked young franchise that included future MVP Kevin Durant and future All-Star Russell Westbrook. The circumstance wasn't one that spelled certain stardom. No matter, Harden made his case as best he could.

In the 2011–12 season, a coming-out year for the bearded wonder, he was named Sixth Man of the Year, the youngest in history.

CAREER HIGHLIGHTS

- Named NBA Sixth Man of the Year for 2011–12
- Has played in three All-Star Games (2013–2015)
- Won an Olympic gold medal with the U.S. men's basketball team in London in 2012
- Led the NBA in free-throw attempts in 2012–13 and 2013–2014
- Led the NBA in total points in 2014–15

Harden's presence off the bench was a massive factor in the Thunder's reaching the NBA Finals that season. A .491 shooting percentage, coupled with 39 percent from behind the arc, meant All-Star-level production coming off the bench for Oklahoma. In terms of advanced stats, he finished second that year in true shooting percentage and effective shooting percentage. Problem was, after a finals loss to the Miami Heat, there was simply no way Oklahoma could keep Harden as well as starters Durant and Westbrook. Unable to offer Harden the "franchise player" money he deserved heading into the 2012–13 season, the Thunder dealt the talented guard to the Rockets, where he's become the backbone of the team and a

centerpiece for an offense that relies heavily on the three-point shot.

What did Harden do once he got to Houston? He started with a first game for the ages: 37 points, 12 assists, 6 rebounds and 4 steals. He continued his stellar play and made his first All-Star appearance. He posted a 45-point night and his first triple-double and finished the year as the fifth highest scorer in the NBA (25.9 points per game). He led the league in free throws attempted and was second in free throws made. And all this after helping Team USA to Olympic gold in 2012. Was he worth $80 million over five years? It certainly looked like it.

Following the addition of Dwight Howard the Rockets have soared, finishing 2013–14 with a 54-28 record. But matched against the Damian Lillard–led Portland Trail Blazers, the Rockets lost a heartbreaker of a Game 6 in the first round of the playoffs when Lillard dropped a buzzer-beating three to end the series. Harden averaged 27 points per game in the losing effort.

Harden doesn't just score, he impacts the entire game when he's on the court. Using his lethal Eurostep, the left-handed dribbler drives to the basket, where he's one of the NBA's top players in drawing fouls.

It doesn't hurt that he hits nearly 9 out of 10 free throws, and in one game this past season, he went 21 for 22 from the line. And although he may not be the league's top assist man, with defenders worried more about his speed to the basket and his killer crossover, Harden's excelled at finding open teammates waiting behind the arc to drop a trey. The 2014–15 season was good to Harden. He led the league in total points (2,217), was second in points per game (27.37) and was first in free throws made and attempted; his total of 715 made free throws was more than the next player had even attempted. He finished ninth overall in assists per game (6.98), and he's not even a true point guard. He's improved his defense, increasing his rebounds, steals and blocks per game, and has established himself as an MVP candidate, finishing second overall in voting after the 2014–15 season.

The gregarious shooting guard, whose beard has its own Twitter account, is thriving with the weight of the Rockets' offense on his shoulders. In just a few short years he's become one of the best players in the world, and if he brings a championship to Houston, he'll live on with Rockets legends like Moses Malone and Hakeem Olajuwon.

LEBRON JAMES 23

FEW BASKETBALL PLAYERS define an era. But when they do, they're often known by a single name. Kareem. Bird. Magic. Jordan. And the man who has ushered basketball into the 21st century is known simply as LeBron.

LeBron James was born on the second last day of 1984 in Akron, Ohio. His mother was just 16 years old, and the two bounced around from apartment to apartment as his mother sought work. By his junior year of high school, he was the most famous teen athlete in the United States, appearing on the cover of *Sports Illustrated* and wowing the nation with his unique blend of size, speed and athleticism. When the Cleveland Cavaliers made him the number one overall pick in the 2003 NBA Draft, he was already more famous than Bird, Magic or Jordan were at that stage in their careers. One writer called James "the most hyped basketball player ever."

Football-player big at 6-foot-8 and 250 pounds, James immediately made an impact on the NBA as an 18-year-old in 2003–04, dropping 25 points in his first game. Despite his Cavs missing the playoffs, a new era had begun. James was the automatic choice for Rookie of the Year, and in his second season, LeBron started making magic. He scorched the Toronto Raptors for

56 points, and he posted four games of 40 points or more and a staggering 22 games with 30 points or more—astonishing numbers for someone just 20 years old.

Although he led the league in scoring in 2007–08 with 30 points per game, the 2008–09 season may have been LeBron's best. He led the Cavs in the five major statistical categories en route to a 66-16 record. But a third-round exit at the hands of the Orlando Magic ruined hopes of a title to cap off his MVP-winning year. Lack of success in Cleveland weighed on James. Thus came his move to Miami and the ill-

fated television special he produced—*The Decision*—to announce it. Opting out of his contract with Cleveland and signing with the Miami Heat for the 2010–11 season allowed James to form a mini-dynasty with Chris Bosh and Dwyane Wade, his fellow draftees from 2003. *The Decision* was a PR disaster, despite the millions he raised for charity, and the shine of LeBron's sparkling career appeared to dull in the wake of his commitment to Miami. In terms of legacy making, however, he accomplished his goal, reaching the finals four times in a row during his tenure with the Heat, winning twice, and twice more he was named MVP to go along with the two he earned in Cleveland. But with an opt-out clause, James controlled his own destiny, choosing to return to Cleveland in 2014–15 as the prodigal son.

Everyone wondered if the fans would embrace him—they burned his jersey when he first turned his back on the city. But success has a funny way of changing things. With Kyrie Irving and Kevin Love as his new right-hand men, LeBron began eyeing the next challenge. His first triple-double of the season in early November—a 32-12-10 effort against New Orleans—turned around a sluggish start for Cleveland's new trio, and the

Cavaliers finally found a rhythm, coasting to a 53-29 record. LeBron finished the year with averages of 25.3 points, 6 rebounds and 7.4 assists.

He one-upped even himself in the playoffs. Missing Love to injury during the second round, the Cavs dispatched the Bulls in six games with LeBron averaging 26 points, 11 boards and 8.8 assists over the series. Cleveland then coasted past the Hawks, and by Game 1 of the finals against the Golden State Warriors, it was just LeBron and a cast of secondary characters after Irving succumbed to a broken kneecap.

He threw up more shots in the first two games than anyone ever has, scoring 44 in a Game 1 loss and recording a triple-double in Game 2, both of which went to overtime. In a Game 5 loss, he recorded a 40-point triple-double. Despite putting up MVP-like numbers on a losing team, LeBron wasn't named finals MVP: it was Golden State's Andre Iguodala who took home the award, mostly for guarding LeBron. James finished the series averaging 35.8 points, 13.3 rebounds and 8.8 assists, the first player in finals history to lead both teams in all major statistical categories.

Not yet 30, LeBron is a 10-time All-Star, four-time MVP, two-time finals MVP and three-time Olympic medalist. His career numbers undoubtedly put him in the upper echelon of anyone who has ever played the game of basketball. He cracked the top 20 all-time scoring list in 2014–15 and may be the only man on the planet to have a shot at dethroning Kareem Adbul-Jabbar's record. He may not be the purest scorer, strongest rebounder or most efficient playmaker, but he may go down as the most complete basketball player the world has ever seen.

CAREER HIGHLIGHTS

- Named NBA Most Valuable Player four times (2008–09, 2009–10, 2011–12, 2012–13)
- Named MVP of the NBA Finals twice (2011–12, 2012–13)
- Named the All-Star Game MVP twice (2005–06, 2007–08)
- Won an Olympic gold medal with the U.S. men's basketball team in Beijing in 2008 and London in 2012
- Is the active NBA points-per-game leader (27.3)

CHRIS PAUL 3

IF YOU WANT a smooth, pure basketball player who makes playing in the NBA look easy and who is a true gentleman on and off the court, look no further than Chris Paul, the cornerstone of the Los Angeles Clippers franchise.

Ever since winning Rookie of the Year for his stellar 2005–06 campaign, there has been no stopping the ascent of the 6-foot guard. He's a team leader and a pass-first guard whose effusive charm, wide smile and hustle on the court have earned him accolades as one of the most respected players in the league.

The product of Wake Forest, Paul spent two years running the floor for the Demon Deacons, averaging 15 points and 6.3 assists per game before declaring for the 2005 draft, where he was taken fourth overall by the New Orleans Hornets.

It wasn't until his third year (2007–08) that Paul led the Hornets to the playoffs, and that season he exceeded the already high expectations placed on him. Paul led the NBA in assists (925), assists per game (11.6), steals (217) and steals per game (2.7) while knocking down 21.1 points per contest. His dominance on both ends of the floor had him second in MVP voting to the LA Lakers' Kobe Bryant. The Hornets also won their only playoff series to date that year, a 4-1 romp over the Dallas Mavericks in which Paul destroyed Jason Kidd in their 1-on-1 matchup, while recording three double-doubles in the series and a

triple-double in the final game.

But Paul's time with the Hornets was short-lived. With no supporting cast, and not wanting to play in the basement, Paul asked to be dealt, leading to the most famous NBA trade that never happened.

Commissioner David Stern, in a completely unprecedented move, vetoed a deal that

28

would have sent Paul to the Lakers to join Kobe Bryant, a dream scenario that never manifested. Subsequently, days later, Paul was shipped to the Clippers. There, he teamed with Blake Griffin to form a duo equally formidable to the Paul–Bryant pipe dream, and the Clippers are now a marquee franchise on par with the Lakers.

Paul's a perennial leader in the assist category. Four times he's led the league, most recently with back-to-back seasons of 10.7 dimes (2013–14) and 10.2 (2014–15). He's a dish-first point guard who looks for backdoor cuts, trailing big men or plays off the pick and roll. But don't mistake him for an average shooter—he's lethal with an open-look jumper. Paul is creative off the dribble, he possesses a killer crossover, and with the Clippers, he has developed out-of-this world aerial chemistry with the super-talented Griffin. The Clippers' nickname, "Lob City," didn't come about by accident.

And what's become apparent in Los Angeles is that Paul may be best as a Robin, not a Batman. He's still a strong court general—always probing new ways to the basket, posing as a threat to pass, shoot, lob or penetrate deep into the key. The Clippers point guard is the fulcrum of one of the best offenses in the league, and he is solid on D too.

Paul has six times led the league in steals, including four straight (2010–11 to 2013–14). You'd be hard-pressed to find someone not refer to Paul as the best defensive point guard in the NBA. To illustrate his balanced play, he's been a first- or second-team choice as All-NBA and All-Defensive NBA for seven of his 10 seasons.

Where Paul's critics slam him is in the postseason. But given his performance in Game 7 of the first round of the 2015 playoffs against the San Antonio Spurs, that tune will start to change. Fighting through a hamstring injury, Paul drove to the hoop past Danny Green and hit a last-second off-balance, off-the glass winner over friend Tim Duncan to send the Clips to the next round and their fans into a frenzy. It was easily the biggest shot of his career

and should silence those who claim Paul isn't clutch. But the Clips still managed to blow a 3-1 lead in the second round to the Houston Rockets, and Paul, despite playing his guts out, failed to reach a conference finals once again.

He's already cracked the top 20 in all-time assists and will likely go down not only as the greatest point guard of his generation but as one of the best to ever grace the floor. For Paul, only a championship will burnish his legacy further.

CAREER HIGHLIGHTS

- Named NBA Rookie of the Year for 2005–06
- Named the All-Star Game MVP in 2012–13
- Won an Olympic gold medal with the U.S. men's basketball team in Beijing in 2008 and London in 2012
- Is the active NBA assist-per-game leader (9.9)
- In 10 seasons has led the NBA in steals six times and assists four times

CHICAGO BULLS

POSITION POINT GUARD / **SHOOTS** RIGHT / **HEIGHT** 6'3" / **WEIGHT** 190 LB. / **DRAFTED** 2008, CHICAGO BULLS, 1ST OVERALL

DERRICK ROSE 1

INJURIES CAN DERAIL the best athletes. Some never recover, and their careers are forever marked with an asterisk. So maybe the true sign of a superstar is in his ability to come back—not just as a shadow of the player he once was, but at his peak level.

It is this standard Derrick Rose is trying to achieve, three years removed from a

torn ACL that halted the former MVP in his tracks. And while everyone agrees the talent is there to call him the best in the world, Rose will have to prove he can stay healthy if wants to continue earning the moniker in the future.

Former teammate Kyle Korver said of Rose's comeback in 2015 that he looked

"stronger and more explosive." He went on to explain how important Rose is to Bulls fans and the city of Chicago. As a hometown kid, Rose grew up in the shadow of Michael Jordan's success, and now the 26-year-old is seen as the franchise's savior.

Maybe it's where he's from, Englewood, one of the most crime-ridden neighborhoods in America. Rose's older brother Randall acted like a father, protecting the next big thing in basketball, and easily the greatest thing to ever come out of Chicago's South Side. He torched the basketball scene for Simeon High, and in his senior year put up 25.1 points per game, 9.1 rebounds and 8.8 assists en route to being named to the McDonald's All-American team.

Rose earned a scholarship to Memphis and as a freshman led the Tigers all the way to the 2008 NCAA championship game, losing to Kansas in overtime despite pouring in 17 points, 6 rebounds and 7 assists. That summer he was drafted first overall by the Bulls.

He quickly made a name for himself in the NBA, claiming 2008–09 Rookie of the Year honors, dropping 16.3 points per game and adding 6.3 assists. Then, in his playoff debut against the Boston Celtics, Rose put up a 35-spot against the reigning league champs.

At 22, he was crowned the NBA's MVP, the youngest player to ever hold the honor. His numbers that year (2010–11) were

CAREER HIGHLIGHTS

- Named NBA Most Valuable Player for 2010–2011
- Named NBA Rookie of the Year for 2008–09
- Named an NBA All-Rookie (First Team) in 2008–09
- Has played in three All-Star Games (2010–2012)
- Is a five-time NBA Player of the Week and two-time NBA Player of the Month

semifinals. He was the toast of the league, a slashing point guard capable of amazing reverse layups. At 6-foot-3, he possessed a perfect blend of size, speed and talent. But 11 months later, he blew out his left knee; surgery to repair a torn ACL would sideline him for the remainder of the 2011–12 season and all of the 2012–13 season.

But he eventually came back, and with all the time off it is difficult to think that maybe it was too fast. In 2013–14 he registered just 10 games before the meniscus in his right knee failed him. Another season-ending injury and more questions. Would he ever be the same?

The Bulls kept churning, and as one of the more well-rounded teams in the league—led by Joakim Noah in Rose's absence—they were a midlevel squad, but they definitely missed Rose. Taking some of the burden off of Rose's knees in 2014–15 was paramount. With the addition of All-Star center Pau Gasol, and the emergence of Jimmy Butler in Rose's backcourt, Rose was no longer the single driving force of the offense.

And he finally found his game in 2015. Hampered by lingering injuries and possible fatigue at the start of the season, Rose eventually picked up the pace. In January, he scored 20.3 points per game, averaged 4.9 assists and, most importantly, played an average of 34 minutes. Heading into the All-Star break against the then-surging Cleveland Cavaliers, Rose dropped 30 against LeBron in a 113–98 blowout. Any celebrations were short-lived, however. In late February, the Bulls announced Rose had torn the same meniscus in his right knee and would be lost for some time. He valiantly returned late in the season, playing in all of the Bulls' playoff games and averaging more than 37 minutes and 20 points, but the Bulls fell short, succumbing to the Cleveland Cavaliers in the second round.

It was a treat seeing the old Rose, flying through the air again, hanging for an extra second and flipping the ball in the hoop past helpless defenders, just like he always did. No one doubts his character. Just his body.

impressive of course—25 points per game, 7.7 assists, 4.1 boards and a free-throw percentage over 85 percent, all but the assists being career highs. The Bulls amassed the best record in the NBA with 60 wins, and Rose led the team deep into the Eastern Conference finals—their first trip there since 1998—but they eventually succumbed to the Miami Heat. Rose, for his part, averaged 27.1 points and 7.7 assists over 16 games, including a 44-point performance against the Atlanta Hawks in the conference

POSITION SHOOTING GUARD–POINT GUARD / **SHOOTS** RIGHT / **HEIGHT** 6'4" / **WEIGHT** 220 LB. / **DRAFTED** 2003, MIAMI HEAT, 5TH OVERALL

DWYANE WADE ³

FEW GUARDS IN recent memory have had an impact on the game like Dwyane Wade. A slasher, a shooter, a leader, Wade's combined attributes have made him what all athletes aspire to be called: a winner.

He didn't have the easiest upbringing on the South Side of Chicago, with a mother in and out of jail and suffering from addiction issues. He turned to sports, thriving on both the basketball court and the football field. In his senior year, he dropped a cool 27 points and 11 rebounds on average as a starting shooting guard for Harold L. Richards High School in Oak Lawn, Illinois.

Wade spent two years at Marquette before leapfrogging to the NBA. He was drafted fifth overall in the 2003 draft, one of the best on record; the draft included his future teammates LeBron James and Chris Bosh. At Marquette, he was an absolute stud, averaging 19.7 points a game and racking up 150 steals and 79 blocked shots over two seasons. But the highlight was his triple-double (only the fourth in NCAA history at that point) against number one ranked Kentucky in the 2003 NCAA tournament, vaulting Marquette into the Final Four for the first time since 1977.

"D-Wade" has since spent his entire career in Miami, winning three titles. But perhaps the first one is the most memorable—it certainly marked Wade's arrival as a bona fide superstar. In just his third season, Wade dropped 27.2 points a game in the regular season, adding 6.7

assists and 5.7 rebounds, some serious numbers from the two-guard position. The Heat soared through the playoffs but found themselves down 0-2 in the finals to Dirk Nowitzki and the Dallas Mavericks. The

Heat fought back, winning four straight. Wade dropped over 40 points in both Games 3 and 5, battling through injuries, and he was named 2006 finals MVP.

Wade missed large chunks of the next

two seasons with injuries, but he still managed to help the 2008 men's U.S. Olympic team win gold. But once healthy again, he dominated the NBA. In the 2008–09 season, he led the NBA in scoring, putting up 30.2 points per game, setting career highs in assists with 7.5 and steals with 2.2 per contest. But the Heat were ousted in seven against the Hawks, and things were about to change.

Wade's career with the Heat turned a corner when he helped persuade James and Bosh to leave Cleveland and Toronto, respectively, and join him in Miami. All three belonged to the same draft class and thus had expiring contracts. The move tipped the balance of players' working contracts to their favor rather than general managers always dictating the terms.

The trio formed an unstoppable presence in South Beach, making four trips in a row to the NBA Finals, winning twice. It wasn't the multiple rings that James boasted they would win when they announced their decision during the summer of 2010, but it was enough for the rest of the league to take notice—the Heat were the team to beat for four years, and in the modern cap era, as close to a dynasty as it gets.

Wade and Bosh remained in Miami for the 2014–15 season, bidding adieu to LeBron, who returned to Cleveland. But both Bosh and Wade, who amassed major playoff minutes over the years, were hampered by injuries, and the Heat failed to make the playoffs despite stalwart efforts by both. Wade for his part averaged 21.5 points in 62 games, adding 4.8 assists and 3.5 off the glass.

Where Wade goes next is anybody's guess—he's only played for one team but is likely headed to free agency, where he can add star power and a few more good years to any contending team. It'll have to be a team where he handles the ball, though—although Wade may have some miles, the shooting guard isn't quite resigned to a backup veteran role just yet, and he's more like Kobe in that he's going to need the rock. He can still drive to the basket and nail his off-balance shots; he can still cross

over with the best of them and pull up for the J; and his mere presence on the court is enough to make a young guard quiver on the defensive end. Off the court, he's been a role model, active in charitable events and one of the most bankable and brandable superstars in the league.

He's one of the league's good guys. And with three rings, he's proven that he's not only a winner but a fighter, too; he's won as top dog and as a supporting star. He's a classic example of a team-first superstar.

CAREER HIGHLIGHTS

- Named MVP of the NBA Finals in 2005–06
- Named the All-Star Game MVP in 2009–10
- Has played in 11 All-Star Games (2005–2015)
- Won an Olympic gold medal with the U.S. men's basketball team in Beijing in 2008
- Was the NBA scoring champion in 2008–09

POSITION POINT GUARD / **SHOOTS** RIGHT / **HEIGHT** 6'3" / **WEIGHT** 200 LB. / **DRAFTED** 2008, SEATTLE SUPERSONICS, 4TH OVERALL

RUSSELL WESTBROOK⁰

IT WAS HARD to tell what the Oklahoma Thunder (formerly the Seattle SuperSonics) acquired with the fourth overall pick in the 2008 draft when they selected Russell Westbrook. He didn't shine in high school until his senior year, when he averaged 25.1 points per game and grabbed 8.7 rebounds as a point guard playing for Leuzinger High School in Long Beach, California. One thing was certain though: he made his basketball teams better. Twice, UCLA made the Final Four with Westbrook in the backcourt, and during his last year with the Bruins before declaring for the NBA Draft he posted 12.7 points, 3.7 rebounds and 4.9 assists. But was that any indicator he would become one of the most feared men in the NBA?

His first coach certainly knew, commenting in 2011 upon Westbrook's first All-Star Game: "Russell . . . wasn't distracted by anything. He had a vision at a young age of what he wanted to do and where he wanted to get." His father, Russell Sr., also knew—or at least ensured a strong work ethic that would become the backbone of Westbrook's game, as the protégé would take 500 shots per day in the gym and do countless sit-ups and push-ups. Despite being undersized, Westbrook had a reputation for being the toughest and hardest-working player on the court.

That work ethic continued when he arrived in Oklahoma, joining heralded small forward Kevin Durant to form one of the NBA's best one-two combos. But Westbrook began largely in Durant's shadow as the Thunder established itself as a contender in the tough Western Conference. It's no slight—Durant is a former MVP, a four-time scoring champ, a six-time All-Star and one of the greatest superstars in the league. So for Westbrook to become as formidable a force as Durant is incredible.

CAREER HIGHLIGHTS

His rookie season, Westbrook put home a solid 15.1 points per game, along with 4.9 rebounds, 5.3 assists and 1.3 steals. By his third year, he'd increased almost every one of those totals en route to a first All-Star appearance—21.9 points, 4.6 rebounds, 8.2 assists and nearly 2 steals per game. That season he posted a career-high 45 points versus the Minnesota Timberwolves and helped lead the Thunder to their first NBA Finals appearance—losing in five games to the Miami Heat. In 2013–14, Westbrook shone in the playoffs despite Oklahoma's six-game loss in the conference finals to the San Antonio Spurs. The point guard absolutely commanded the floor, averaging a whopping 26.7 points, 8.1 rebounds and 7.3 assists during the series—the last guy to be that good across those metrics was named Oscar Robertson—and Westbrook finally felt like a household name.

In just seven seasons he's already hit double digits in career triple-doubles. He's one of the most versatile guards in the game. He can hurt opposing teams in a variety of ways, whether it be attacking the hoop, dropping a 15-footer—his "cotton shot"—or passing to a cutting big man like Serge Ibaka. Although Westbrook may not be a reliable three-point threat, his tough-as-nails defense makes up for his lack of deep scoring.

And although the dynamic duo running the lanes amid the plains of Oklahoma City haven't won a championship yet, many can feel it coming. The 2014–15 season was a speed bump, though. Durant suffered a broken foot during the preseason, and Westbrook followed that up with a broken hand several games in—the Thunder were behind the eight ball from the get-go. But a turning point came in mid-December versus the Cleveland Cavaliers. Coming into the game 8-13, with Westbrook and Durant both finally back, they combined for 45 points and it finally felt like the old championship-caliber Thunder. And Westbrook continued his dominance, delivering a 31-point, 10-assist performance soon after in a win versus the LA Lakers. With Durant out of the lineup again in late February, Westbrook posted back-to-back

- Named the All-Star Game MVP in 2014–15
- Named an NBA All-Rookie (First Team) in 2008–09
- Won an Olympic gold medal with the U.S. men's basketball team in London in 2012
- Led the league in points per game in 2014–15 (28.1)
- Is a 10-time NBA Player of the Week

triple-doubles, including 39 points, 14 boards, 11 dimes and 3 steals in an overtime loss to the Phoenix Suns. Over a four-game stretch, Westbrook became the first player since Michael Jordan to post four straight triple-doubles, capping it off with a 49-point, 16 rebound, 12 assist outburst against the Philadelphia 76ers.

It's coming, that trip back to the finals. And if anyone is going to ensure it happens, it's the hardworking point guard from Long Beach, no longer in the shadows of Durant but standing alongside the MVP, making a case that it may have been his team all along.

THE NBA DRAFT

BOOM OR BUST IN '84

In 1984, the Portland Trail Blazers selected Sam Bowie second overall, one spot behind Hakeem "the Dream" Olajuwon and one position ahead of a guard from North Carolina named Michael Jordan. In hindsight, how anyone could pass up the greatest basketball player of all time may seem baffling, almost unconscionable. It's why to this day the 1984 draft is the most scrutinized, perhaps the most famous draft class of all time. That's not because of Jordan—it's because of Bowie.

At the time, Jordan's going third made sense. Guards were not seen as focal points of basketball teams in the 70s and 80s—big men like Bill Walton, Julius Erving and Kareem Abdul-Jabbar were—and players like Jordan and Magic Johnson had yet to make a full impact on the psyche of executives and fans during the 80s. The 1984 draft in many ways became a tipping point for a new NBA.

A series of unusual circumstances sent Bowie—the greatest high school player of his era—to Portland. The Trail Blazers selected

Sam Bowie, left, and Hakeem Olajuwon flank NBA commissioner David Stern follwing the 1984 draft.

future All-Star Clyde Drexler at the guard position in 1983—he declared before his senior year to enter the '83 draft—so with no need for another backcourt presence, Portland had set their sights beyond Jordan well before the executives gathered in Madison Square Garden for the '84 draft.

Portland, well aware of Bowie's progress, and unhappy with their center Tom Owens, traded the underperforming big to Indiana in June of 1981 in exchange for Indiana's number one pick in '84. Luckily for Portland, the Pacers finished dead last in the East in 1983–84, positioning the Blazers in what became a two-horse race for a game-changing player with the West's worst team, the Houston Rockets. The fate of both franchises came down to a simple coin toss for the number one pick (the draft lottery didn't begin until 1985).

Houston won the flip, and as they say, the rest is history.

By choosing Olajuwon, Drexler's college teammate in Houston, the Rockets got an immensely talented Nigerian-born center who'd taken his college team to back-to-back NCAA finals. Portland's consolation prize was Bowie. The Trail Blazers' prior success with another pass-heavy big man, Bill Walton, weighed heavily in the minds of management prior to the 1984 draft. They needed a center to complement Drexler, not another guard. So they chose big, passing over Jordan.

The debate still rages: do you take the most talented player in the draft, regardless of position, or do you fill a need? Mind you, if Bowie hadn't been injured in college, redshirted and played an extra fifth year, he might have gone number one in '83, and the whole Jordan fiasco would have been prevented. (Olajuwon also redshirted a year upon arrival in the U.S.) Another NBA-ready center, Patrick Ewing, who defeated Olajuwon in the 1984 NCAA finals, remained for his senior season at Georgetown. Drafted first overall in 1985, imagine how insane a draft with Ewing, Bowie, and Olajuwon would have been. Hindsight is 20/20, but one wonders if Bowie's career trajectory would have been different as well if Drexler hadn't declared early and Ewing hadn't declared late. An even greater urban myth (at least according to Olajuwon's autobiography) persists that Portland nearly traded Drexler and the second overall pick to Houston for Ralph Sampson. Meaning the Rockets would have ended up with Jordan, Drexler and Olajuwon—one of those three played in an NBA Finals every season from 1990 to 1998 with their respective teams.

WHO WAS SAM Bowie, and how did he become the biggest bust of all time? A 7-foot-1 high school phenom from Lebanon, Pennsylvania, Bowie, as a junior, took his team all the way to the state final before losing by one point. In his senior year in 1979 he averaged 28.8 points per game. Few centers his size could run the floor with grace and agility at such a young age; few could pass like a guard and post

Sam Bowie of Kentucky hauls down a rebound against Georgetown in the 1984 NCAA tournament.

like a big. Bowie was so legendary in high school, he signed autographs everywhere he went with the signature "the Million Dollar Kid." His face was plastered on the cover of sports sections across the country, including the cover of *Sports Illustrated*. For a time, it's not an overstatement to say that Bowie was the most famous basketball player on the planet. Four hundred colleges contacted the teenager—he eventually chose the University of Kentucky. But injuries in college caused Bowie to miss nearly two years of basketball after a broken leg was left untreated and never healed properly. By the time he reached the NBA Draft in 1984, moments away from realizing his lifelong dream and cashing in big time, he had buckled under the pressure. In 2012, for an ESPN documentary, Bowie revealed he lied to the Trail Blazers about the pain in his leg prior to the draft. When the Portland medical team tapped on his tibia during a physical, Bowie said, "I can still remember them taking a little mallet, and when they would hit me on my left tibia . . . I would tell 'em, 'I don't feel anything.' But deep down inside, it was hurting." Desperate to achieve his NBA dream, he went on to say he did what anyone would have done in his position, and one can't help but look back tragically at a man hanging on to a fading dream.

A 17-year-old Kobe Bryant is all smiles after the post-draft trade that sent him from Charlotte to Los Angeles.

Greg Oden. Taken first overall by the Trail Blazers in 2007, Oden's been injured most of his career and hasn't made an impact for any team. Even worse, the Blazers could have had Kevin Durant that year, an heir apparent to Jordan, and in many ways, Oden/Durant is the mirror image of Bowie/Jordan.

Drafts are funny things. The '84 draft was in fact loaded with talent beyond the top three picks, but it's forever become known for the three major players—Olajuwon, Bowie, Jordan. But future Hall of Famers like Charles Barkley (the fifth overall pick) and John Stockton (selected 16th!) get easily forgotten under the shadow of Jordan and company. Even Sam Perkins and Kevin Willis had long, serviceable NBA careers, providing more ammunition in the argument for deepest draft on record. But the latter two have become footnotes in history. Booms and busts are what make a draft memorable—1984 just happened to have both.

THE KIDS ARE ALL RIGHT, SOMETIMES

Ask fans to name the 13th pick overall in 1996 and they might be hard-pressed to come up with the name Kobe Bryant. Or two picks later, if you were to ask who was drafted 15th overall, would they be able to recall the greatest Canadian import in the history of the NBA, Steve Nash? That same draft was littered with future stars—Allen

Bowie actually posted decent numbers his rookie season in the NBA—10 points per game, 8.6 rebounds—but another broken leg the following year began a long streak of tibial fractures, this time to his right leg, derailing his once promising career, and the "bust" talk began in earnest. At the same time, Jordan was taking off, en route to championship after championship, dropping 40-plus with regularity while Bowie sat on the sidelines helplessly for more than two years. (Jordan, famously competitive, took distinct pleasure in torching Portland over the years for passing him over.) Bowie finally retired in 1995, averaging 10.9 points per game, 7.5 boards and nearly 2 blocks per contest over his career, not horrible numbers by any means, but for the man drafted before Jordan, for the man who played on two broken legs, those numbers will never be good enough.

Inexplicably, Portland factored into another great draft bust,

Iverson first overall, guards Peja Stojakovic (14th) and Derek Fisher (24th), and centers Jermaine O'Neal (17th) and Zydrunas Ilgauskas (20th). Although '84 may possess a plethora of Hall of Famers and an enticing story, '96 counts itself as one of the greatest drafts simply for the sheer number of men who went on to long, potent careers—and three future MVPs.

Was it something in the water that year? Why do certain draft classes produce an inordinate number of NBA-ready stars? Basketball players enter the league at different points in their high school or college careers and enter the draft at various stages in their development. Some commit to four-year college programs and enter the NBA at 21 years of age, while others, like LeBron James—a man by the time he was able to drive—skip postsecondary schooling altogether and enter the league at just 18. (This ended after the 2005 draft, when

Philadelphia's Allen Iverson drives past a trio of Toronto Raptors, including rookie Chris Bosh (left), in 2003.

or 13 is an advantage that allows those children to excel through the higher levels of the system.)

The 1996 draft class has been called one of the best of all time, with Bryant, Nash and Iverson all going on to win the MVP award—that's by far the most successful group of individuals out of any class. Future stars such as Stephon Marbury and Ray Allen went fourth and fifth, respectively. One can't help but think what the fate of the two Canadian expansion franchises, Toronto and Vancouver, might have been had they not chosen Marcus Camby and Shareef Abdur-Rahim at two and three in '96. Can you imagine being one of the GMs who passed on Bryant, Nash, Allen and Marbury? Camby and Abdur-Rahim turned out to be serviceable NBA players, but certainly not MVPs or All-Stars.

A legit number one can change a city. The aforementioned Iverson took Philly from joke squad to legit contender, making the NBA Finals in 2001. Kobe, however, became part of Phil Jackson's next big thing. His long-term consistency would have made any team better, but perhaps the hardest thing to gauge beyond talent is whether an 18- or 19-year-old has the mental fortitude, stamina and leadership

the league mandated that a player must turn 19 no later than December 31 of the year of the draft and be at least one year removed from high school graduation.)

A common refrain nowadays is "one-and-dones," players who possess the physical talent to play in the NBA at just 19 years of age and suit up for just one year of college. The 2014 first overall pick—and subsequent 2015 Rookie of the Year—Andrew Wiggins, did just that. He played one year at Kansas, a school dedicated to shaping one-and-dones, before abdicating to the NBA. If not for the rule change, he may have been a high school declarant.

There's no magic potion for why '96 or '84 exists, no Malcolm Gladwell moment to fall back on. (Gladwell argues that for hockey players, month of birth determines future success for NHLers because at certain age levels, kids are grouped together by birth month, and an inordinate number of NHL players are born in the first six months of the year, and being older/faster/stronger at 12

skills to keep winning at a high level. For all the Bryants out of high school, there is a Jonathan Bender (fifth overall, Toronto, 1999), Darius Miles (third overall, LA Clippers, 2000) and DeSagana Diop (eighth overall, Cleveland, 2001)—all of them massive mistakes that have haunted those GMs for years.

For all the research, talent assessment, scouting and hand-wringing that go into drafting, how do so many teams get it wrong? Is it really just luck of the draw? This is what New Jersey Nets coach John Calipari (now head coach of Kentucky) said on draft night in 1996: "We really like Kobe. I think he's gonna be a terrific player in the NBA. But for us, right now, where we are and what we needed, I think in the end, [the right choice] was Kerry Kittles."

His is a common refrain: despite obviously talented players, teams often draft on need, not talent (or at least they used to). The Nets needed a forward that year, not a guard, similar to the Blazers in '84.

Carmelo Anthony, left, Dwyane Wade, center, and Chris Bosh make a media appearance prior to the 2003 NBA Draft. The trio were respectively selected third, fifth and fourth.

In 1996, Philadelphia 76ers GM Brad Greenberg, who had the first overall pick, said at the time that he didn't want a teenager. "I wasn't comfortable going with a [high school] kid for the number one pick vs. Iverson." In hindsight, despite Iverson's brilliance, he chose wrong when you consider the longevity of Bryant's career and what he's meant to the Lakers. Iverson ended up doing wonders revitalizing the Philly basketball market, but he flamed out before winning anything substantial. Bryant went on to five rings. In the end, the 76ers missed out on a once-in-a-generation talent and a future Hall of Famer, but would they have done it differently?

It's important to remember that drafting an 18-year-old out of high school in the mid-90s was less common and ultimately seen as a gamble. When Minnesota took a teenaged Kevin Garnett fifth overall in 1995, it was seen as backwards thinking rather than as trendsetting.

Garnett proved his naysayers wrong and went on to have a spectacular career, but one without a championship for Minnesota. Yet he paved the way for Dwight Howard, LeBron and other high schoolers who made the jump to the association.

FAST-FORWARD TO 2003—a draft that rivals '96 and '84 in talent level. The draft had an immediate short-term talent impact on the NBA as well as a long-term one that would change the course of the NBA landscape, specifically in how teams are built and how teams win championships. Number one that year was a gimme. LeBron James was as automatic as they come, the greatest high schooler ever, a football player's build in a basketball player's body, and the hope was he would be a franchise changer for his hometown of Cleveland. Next pick—the only misstep of the top five—was Darko Milicic. The following three—Carmelo Anthony, Chris Bosh and

Derrick Rose playing in 2014. Chicago, who chose Rose first overall in 2008, had a 1.7 percent chance of winning the first pick at that year's draft. If the odds held up, Chicago would have wound up with the ninth overall pick in 2008.

Dwyane Wade—became Olympians and All-Stars, and for Bosh, Wade and James, future champions with the Miami Heat twice over. It's the best top five ever seen, even inclusive of Milicic, and surely better than Jordan's draft year.

But more important is what happened later in their careers. When James and Bosh both opted out of their contracts to join Wade in 2010, a new era began in the NBA, one where players were suddenly mindful of taking control of their own destiny in a salary cap era. It was the ultimate recognition that no one individual can win a ring. James applied the same approach to team building when he rejoined the Cavaliers in 2014, opting out of his contract in Miami to sign with Cleveland. He was instrumental in convincing the brass to trade their number one pick, Canadian Andrew Wiggins, for Kevin Love. Along with point guard Kyrie Irving, the new trio form a formidable threat that fans in Ohio hope will bring them their first championship in over 40 years.

GAMBLING IN THE LOTTERY ERA

For the first 20 years of the NBA Draft, beginning in 1964, a coin flip decided where a first pick landed. That flip could determine how a franchise might flourish or perish. Heads or tails. Pure luck. A 50/50 chance. But finally, in 1984, the NBA Board of Governors voted to introduce the lottery, a weighted system that gave the worst team in the NBA the greatest chance of securing the number one pick. The league has never looked back, and never has the marriage between ping-pong and basketball been so important to sport.

Fourteen numbered balls—one to fourteen—are stuffed in a drum. One thousand and one combinations exist, and each team in the lottery is assigned a four-number combo. To determine the draft order, four numbers are sucked up through the pipes. Whatever team has that combination wins the pick. The balls are returned, the process is repeated, and since then, the commissioner's familiar refrain can be heard through the rafters of the host city every June. "With the first pick in the NBA Draft, the [LUCKY TEAM NAME] selects . . .

But beyond the obvious number ones that have emerged over the years, GMs are shifting away from drafting positionally and focusing on talent, especially overseas. Draft picks are inherently calculated gambles—small point guard and reigning MVP Steph Curry was taken seventh overall by Golden State—but sometimes they are just total freakin' long shots. Take Bruno Caboclo, the Toronto Raptors' 20th pick in 2014. Few had heard of him outside of a handful of NBA scouts and general managers. Projected to go second round, his selection last year was immediately questioned on social media. Who was this guy? Why would the Raptors blow their first-rounder on such an obscure kid? But GM Masai Ujiri saw something in Caboclo. Long on potential—he has an enormous

7-foot-6 wingspan—the raw rookie represents exactly the type of risk teams are willing to make in a growing international market. Teams aren't focused on drafting a big man like they were in the 80s with Bowie. Size, speed, long arms for defense and a predilection for hitting a three are all more important than a big body in the middle. And with the success of the Spurs—drafting an unknown commodity such as Tony Parker from Europe—teams are more comfortable taking risks with international players, particularly if it doesn't cost them salary while they hone their skills in European basketball leagues. Additionally, there's more parity in talent level than ever before.

Current Cleveland Cavaliers GM David Griffin said at the 2014 draft: "I don't think there's a clear cut number one pick in most drafts. I think when people say that, they have a really strong feeling for one player over another, but there's not necessarily a consensus." The same might be said for lower picks like Caboclo. Ujiri, perhaps worried another general manager would snap up his guy before the second round, weighed the risk and deemed it acceptable. He and the Raptors can now develop the player as they see fit. The reality is most picks don't pan out anyway, and it's likely Caboclo may not be a productive NBA player. But if he is . . . boom. Smartest thing the Raptors ever did.

BOOMS AND BUSTS. That's what sticks in the minds of many as they look back on the greatest drafts in the history of the league. For every Michael Jordan, there's a Sam Bowie. Taken before the greatest basketball player to ever live, Bowie became an unfortunate punch line, a player who could never live up to expectations. Perhaps history has been unkind to him. Or maybe for every Jordan, there are a thousand Sam Bowies, a thousand hopefuls who dream of NBA stardom. The hope and the dream of every NBA executive is choosing the right one.

INTERNATIONAL STARS

TONY PARKER

MILWAUKEE BUCKS

POSITION SMALL FORWARD–SHOOTING GUARD / **SHOOTS** RIGHT / **HEIGHT** 6'11" / **WEIGHT** 217 LB. / **DRAFTED** 2013, MILWAUKEE BUCKS, 15TH OVERALL

GIANNIS ANTETOKOUNMPO 34

WHEN YOU'VE GOT a nickname like "the Greek Freak," there's bound to be something special about the way you play. That's exactly the case with Giannis Antetokounmpo, the Milwaukee Bucks star who is tearing up the NBA with an insane combination of length, speed and talent with the ball.

Born to Nigerian parents but raised in Athens, Antetokounmpo grew up poor and hungry, sharing basketball sneakers with his brother Thanasis—the two even hawked souvenirs to tourists to help pay the bills. "When we were playing basketball, [we forgot] everything that [was] happening to us," Thanasis said in 2014. Giannis, who was scouted at 13, began plying his trade in a low-level second-division Greek league (what one NBA exec deemed "YMCA level") before reaching the pinnacle of basketball. Given his visibility on YouTube it may feel like the 6-foot-11 small forward has been in the NBA for years, but 2014–15 was only the second full season for the 15th overall pick of the 2013 draft, who's since become a human highlight reel night in, night out.

The excitable international budding star recorded his first career double-double several months into his rookie year, going 16 and 10 against the Brooklyn Nets. By January, he was regularly putting up double-digit figures in points, and his minutes were dramatically increasing, a great sign for a rookie who clearly was picking up on the finer points of the game.

Instead of getting buried on the bench, Antetokounmpo was playing 25 to 30 minutes a night for a young Bucks squad focused on creating a winner. For many

fans, their first large-scale introduction to the high-flying Greek was at the 2015 Slam Dunk Contest. The Freak walked out into Madison Square Garden with a procession of flower-haired women and the Greek flag draped over his shoulders—not a shabby entrance. But the competition quickly showed that Antetokounmpo's in-game dunks are more exciting than the uncontested jams thrown down in exhibition.

When it comes to games that count, Antetokounmpo's crafty Eurostep move—sometimes started beyond the free-throw line—allows him to get to the basket quickly and slam on surprised players. His length is nearly impossible to guard, his wingspan stretching like a bird of prey in midflight. Although he may not be a rebounding machine—he's slender and agile, and more a scorer than a defender—he's certainly capable of getting up on the glass and helping out, as evidenced by the 15 boards he pulled down in a loss to the Houston Rockets in February 2015. But he can also be a help defender by launching in the air against smaller players, and he's added more than a block per game to his arsenal, including four stuffs against the Pacers early in 2015. He may not shoot the three yet—a must for big men these days—but those skills will come once he develops the fundamentals needed to stay in the NBA at a high level. And that's happening; just two games after that loss to Houston, the Greek Freak put up 12 points, 9 boards and 8 assists and added 3 steals for one of his most versatile and well-rounded games to date (and a career high in helpers). In early March, Antetokounmpo dropped a career-high 29 points in a loss to New Orleans, proving he possesses the skill set to be a go-to offensive weapon up front.

The Bucks have become a solid playoff-bound team and are building a nucleus around the Greek prodigy, as well as 2014's number two overall pick Jabari Parker and a cast of young players, including guards Michael Carter-Williams and Canadian Tyler Ennis. His 2014–15 per-game line of 12.7 points, 6.7 rebounds, 2.6 assists and 1 block may not be mind-blowing, but he's showing he's capable of big-game play when it's crunch time. He also plays several positions on the court, giving the Bucks a lot of looks depending on their lineup.

CAREER HIGHLIGHTS

Given enough time, Antetokounmpo may launch himself into the conversation as one of the best international players in the history of the game, alongside stalwarts Dirk Nowitzki and Goran Dragic. He's certain to be the best basketball product to ever come out of the tiny island nation of Greece—a once-in-a-generation talent who seems poised to take the basketball world by storm.

- Drafted by the Milwaukee Bucks in the first round (15th overall) in 2013
- Named an NBA All-Rookie (Second Team) in 2013–14
- Led the Bucks in 2013–14 in two-pointers (376)
- Led the Bucks in 2013–14 in free throws (257)
- Named NBA Player of the Week on February 9, 2015

MIAMI HEAT

POSITION POINT GUARD–SHOOTING GUARD / **SHOOTS** LEFT / **HEIGHT** 6'3" / **WEIGHT** 190 LB. / **DRAFTED** 2008, SAN ANTONIO SPURS, 45TH OVERALL

GORAN DRAGIC 7

EUROPE HAS BECOME a hotbed for NBA talent the past decade, and perhaps no player better exemplifies that basketball truly is an international sport than Goran Dragic, who hails from the tiny country of Slovenia, population two million. He's emerged as one of the best guards in the game, and after several successful seasons in Phoenix, he's now the starting point guard for the Miami Heat.

After an injury derailed his budding career on the soccer field, Dragic turned to the hardcourt. He was immediately hooked, waking up at 3:00 a.m. to watch NBA stars such as Michael Jordan and Allen Iverson. In 2012 he said, "Inside my blood, I love basketball." He tore up the Slovenian league as a youngster and helped lead the U-20 team to a gold medal at the 2004 FIBA championship. Dragic was drafted 45th overall in 2008 by the San Antonio Spurs but was quickly swapped to the Suns. He started slowly, coming off the bench his first three seasons in Phoenix. "I was not aggressive enough," he said, looking back at his early years. His coach told him to forget about the mistakes, but it took a while to sink in. He had an especially difficult time dealing with the larger NBA shot-blockers.

Midway through his third season, the Slovenian was moved to Houston, where he earned backup minutes while continuing to put up respectable numbers. The following season, Dragic finally started, and in 66

CAREER HIGHLIGHTS

games that year posted what at that point was his best line—11.7 points per game, 5.3 assists and a career-high 80.5 percent from the stripe.

As a free agent, the point guard returned to Phoenix, where he was given the chance to start—flourishing as one of the top players in the game at his position. His numbers in 2013–14 were a career best; his averages of 20.3 points per game, 5.9 assists and a smooth .505 field goal percentage helped Dragic emerge as one of the purest shooters in the NBA. He was deadly from behind the arc, converting chances at more than 40 percent—and his defense was good too, with 1.4 steals per contest.

Dragic's go-to move is a nearly unstoppable step-back jumper that is difficult to guard effectively. He sets up the shot by dribbling hard right before launching backward off his left foot to give him separation from his defender and a clean look at the bucket. The shot is very similar to that of fellow international star Dirk Nowitzki, who's used it to climb into the NBA's top-10 all-time scorers. It helps that Dragic is a natural

lefty, another difference maker in his game that makes him difficult to defend.

He had several monster games in early December 2014 for the Suns, dropping 34 against the Pacers, and 28 points and 13 dimes against the Mavericks, powering Phoenix to wins in both contests. Nearing the trade deadline, the Suns had a logjam at point guard and ended up dealing Dragic and his younger brother, Zoran (who joined the Suns at the beginning of 2014–15 and played sparingly in his first stint in the NBA), to Miami for picks and veteran role players. Dragic finished the year with 16.3 points per game, 4.5 helpers and 3.5 rebounds, well above his career numbers; in his 26-game sample with Miami, he continued to play well, improving to 80 percent from the stripe and dishing out 5.3 assists per game.

Dragic's shifty moves and pure jumping ability are two assets that will add several different looks to a Heat offense in need of leadership in the backcourt—although budding point guard Shabazz Napier is waiting in the wings, the rookie's had his

- Named NBA Most Improved Player for 2013–14
- Was an All-NBA Third Team selection for 2013–14
- Is a two-time Stankovic Cup champion with Slovenia (2007, 2010)
- Is a member of the NBA's 20-50-40 club (points, FG %, 3PT %)
- Is a two-time NBA Player of the Week

early struggles. Dragic's new five-year, $90-millon contract means he'll be around to provide guidance to Napier while giving the Heat the pure point guard they've been missing since the James/Wade/Bosh years.

The Slovenian star should be fun to watch in Miami and is expected to be the cornerstone of a franchise seeking to capitalize on the final years of Dwyane Wade and Chris Bosh.

For the point guard from across the world, just making it to the NBA is a success story. Competing at the highest level is a whole different ball game.

POSITION CENTER–POWER FORWARD / **SHOOTS** RIGHT / **HEIGHT** 7'0" / **WEIGHT** 250 LB. / **DRAFTED** 2001, ATLANTA HAWKS, 3RD OVERALL

PAU GASOL 16

ONE OF THE best international centers in the game, Spanish native Pau Gasol has helped redefine the position along with another European, Dirk Nowitzki. And while Gasol may not have the step-back three like the German, his post moves are second to none. After a solid first season with the Chicago Bulls (his 15th), Gasol's hoping to add one more ring to his collection as his career winds down.

Growing up in Barcelona, Gasol was a natural. Seven feet tall before his college years, he destroyed all comers with a crafty mix of agility and touch to go along with his size. He received the MVP award in the 2001 Spanish King's Cup and was soon playing for the Spanish national team.

"He totally exploded and took over. It was pretty unbelievable," recalled his younger brother Marc, himself an All-NBA center.

Pau went third overall in the 2001 draft to the Atlanta Hawks, who immediately traded him to the Memphis Grizzlies for Shareef Abdur-Rahim. The entire Gasol family moved to Tennessee. There, Gasol won 2002 Rookie of the Year. He subsequently spent seven seasons with the Grizzlies, the same team Marc now plays for—they were, in fact, traded for each other. Although the Grizz made the playoffs three years in a row, they never advanced past the first round. Pau took the heat in the south for being soft, and after a foot injury at the 2006 FIBA World Championship sidelined him, his play suffered. He was traded in early 2008 to the LA Lakers in a blockbuster deal that changed everything.

From playing 1A and going to 1B behind Kobe Bryant, Pau made a splash in California, winning two titles with the Lakers. His first full year in LA, Gasol was a beast—his 18.9 points and 9.6 rebounds while playing 37 minutes a night gave the Lakers an offensive boost and gave Bryant the room he needed to operate. Gasol posted similar numbers in the playoffs and tasted victory in the finals over the Orlando Magic, besting Dwight Howard down low.

In each of their title runs, Gasol logged 40 minutes a game, and he averaged more than 20 points and 10 rebounds the year the Lakers repeated, with the Barcelona native hauling down 18 boards in the deciding Game 7 versus the Boston Celtics.

But with Bryant winding down and a failed experiment with Steve Nash, Gasol entered free agency in 2014 and elected to take his talents to Chicago where he could team up with former MVP Derrick Rose and former Defensive Player of the Year Joakim Noah.

His first season in Chitown was a rebirth for Gasol. He hauled down nearly 12 rebounds a game, a career high and good for fourth overall in the league. Contributing 18.5 points per game and 2 blocks (ninth best in the NBA) revealed how well he's played at both ends of the floor, particularly with Rose injured at times. Perhaps no better way to describe the center's worth is the league-leading 54 double-doubles he put up while playing against younger, stronger men. He also had the fifth-most assists per game among power forwards, a testament to his adaptability and ability to read the double team when it comes.

Gasol's well known for his cultural pursuits and is highly intelligent off the court. He speaks numerous languages—he and Bryant used to speak Spanish together on the court to confuse opponents—and he maintains a strong interest in medicine, taking after his mother, who is a doctor.

His consistency and durability at 34 are impressive. He's been an All-Star five times, starting alongside his brother in 2015, the first time in the NBA that's ever happened. He can pass, shoot and run the floor gracefully. In the paint, Gasol's difficult to defend against. A smooth midrange jumper,

his strong post-up and up-and-down head fakes give opponents headaches.

He played the fourth-most minutes of any forward in 2014–15, and those who did spend more time on the court are 10 years his junior. Unfortunately, his season came to a disappointing end. Gasol was injured midway through the second round versus the Cleveland Cavaliers and never seemed to regain his footing or his touch when he returned in Game 6. With a healthy Rose, the team has plenty of upside moving forward. Gasol has two rings already—a third, at 35 years of age or more, would cement a legacy.

CAREER HIGHLIGHTS

- Named NBA Rookie of the Year for 2001–02
- Named an NBA All-Rookie (First Team) in 2001–02
- Has played in five All-Star Games (2006, 2009–2011, 2015)
- Won an Olympic silver medal with the Spanish men's basketball team in London in 2012
- Is the all-time leading scorer in Memphis

MANU GINOBILI [20]

IT'S HARD TO imagine a basketball player having an impact in the NBA when he is closer to 40 than 35—especially a shooting guard whose position dictates lots of slashing and driving play. And yet, Argentine star Manu Ginobili, whose body has taken a beating over the years thanks to his style of play, keeps on ticking. He's still pounding the rock inside to Tim Duncan; still driving to the basket and throwing up a prayer before falling to the floor; still stepping off a screen and taking a pass from Tony Parker. As part of the three-headed international triad in San Antonio, Ginobili will go down as one of the most influential international players in the NBA.

Emanuel Ginobili was drafted 57th overall in 1999. The Spurs fleeced the NBA with their international scouting that year, and it wouldn't be the first time or the last. They already had top pick Duncan, selected in 1997 (from the U.S. Virgin Islands), and they identified Parker (of France) several years later deep in the first round. The Spurs would dominate for the next decade with their internationally born trio.

Ginobili was a huge star in his home country before bolting to Italy. There he played with Kinder Bologna and was named the Euroleague Finals MVP in 2000–01 before crossing the pond and getting his first taste of NBA action as a 25-year-old.

He started just five games his rookie season for San Antonio, averaging 7.6 points and 2 assists per game while playing for a deep Spurs squad that finished 60-22. His impact was felt more in the playoffs, and the Argentine offered a skilled weapon off the bench as the Spurs cruised to victory in the 2003 NBA Finals. It would be their first of three NBA championships in five years. In 2004–05, en route to the second ring, Ginobili started 74 games, knocking down per-game totals of 16 points, 4.4 rebounds and 3.9 assists while shooting 80 percent from the stripe and nearly 38 percent from behind the arc. During the title run, he was even better, upping his point total to 20.8 points, proving he could play the game at an elite level and in crunch time.

CAREER HIGHLIGHTS

- Named NBA Sixth Man of the Year for 2007–08
- Named an NBA All-Rookie (Second Team) in 2002–03
- Has played in two All-Star Games (2005, 2011)
- Was twice named Italian League MVP (2001, 2002)
- Won an Olympic gold medal with the Argentine men's basketball team in Athens in 2004 and a bronze in Beijing in 2008

season-high 46 against Cleveland in a 112–105 win on 15-of-20 shooting, 8 of which were three-pointers. Two nights later, he coolly dropped 7 of 9 from behind the arc and finished with 44. It was this ability to get hot and take over games that endeared him to fans and pushed San Antonio over the top when needed. He started just 23 of 74 games yet played 31 minutes per contest on average, which makes that season even more miraculous. He shot 40 percent from three-point land and 86 percent from the charity stripe, dominant numbers in a year following a title win.

Ginobili's no-holds-barred type of guard play—attacking the rim on offense in a controlled yet reckless manner, while his defense is characterized by a scrappy max effort—paved the way for the current era of superstar guards. Would James Harden exist if Ginobili hadn't been allowed to thrive?

All those extra playoff games and hard-fought minutes added a lot of mileage over the years to Ginobili's legs. In 2014–15, it looked as though the 37-year-old may have lost a step, but he was still effective. He played 70 games coming off the bench and a stalwart 20 minutes per contest. The Spurs will have the crafty 6-foot-6 shooting guard for another season as his partners in crime, Duncan and Parker, are also returning for one more go around. The 2014 title will likely be the feather in the cap for the Argentine, but basketball fans have learned to never say never in Texas. The hope for one more championship is what keeps the aging trio going.

Like most of the Spurs, Ginobili's a truly unique player who bucked the trend, proving that south of the equator isn't just for soccer players. With career per-game averages of 14.3 points, 4 assists and 3 rebounds, 83 percent from the line and 37 percent from deep, the numbers don't tell the whole story for Ginobili. At times, there wasn't a man more important to his team, a glue guard who could play both positions and who accumulated four championship rings, two All-Star appearances and the everlasting respect of fans and players alike.

His creativity with the ball is off the charts, from standard behind-the-back passes to between-the-opposing-legs-of-another-player-passes to laser passes off turnovers into the paint. Basically, Ginobili will make you shake your head at his creativity at least once a game.

In 2008 he was named Sixth Man of the Year, putting up 19.5 points per game (a career high) in a season that included back-to-back 37-point efforts early and a

WASHINGTON WIZARDS

POSITION CENTER–POWER FORWARD / **SHOOTS** RIGHT / **HEIGHT** 6'11" / **WEIGHT** 240 LB. / **DRAFTED** 2005, PHOENIX SUNS, 57TH OVERALL

MARCIN GORTAT 4

YOU MAY JUST be noticing Marcin Gortat, the 6-foot-11, 240-pound big man ruling the paint for the Washington Wizards. And that's okay, because until he became a starter in Phoenix in 2011, he was mostly known—or unknown—as the guy who mopped up for Dwight Howard in Orlando.

He played his first four seasons with the Magic, backing up Howard. In his first year he made $400,000 and started just five games, averaging 6.8 minutes. His statistics, as a result, were largely forgettable. But he learned something in Orlando: that playing basketball in the NBA would never get more difficult than the job he had in practice, namely, guarding the behemoth Howard.

"The worst thing that can happen to you is on your team," he said of having to guard the 280-pound force of nature with elbows like rocks that served to toughen up the already sturdy Gortat.

Gortat was born in Lodz, Poland. His father was a boxer who won two Olympic medals (his brother has taken up the family business now), and his mother played volleyball for the Polish national team. Gortat never played college ball in the United States—instead, he mined his craft in the Euroleague playing for the German team Bundesliga for several seasons before joining the NBA full time in 2007–08.

After Gortat was traded to Phoenix in 2011, he flourished as a starter, and in his first full season in the Sun Belt, he posted

CAREER HIGHLIGHTS

- Drafted by the Phoenix Suns in the second round (57th overall) in 2005
- Is a three-time BBL Cup champion (2004, 2005, 2007)
- Set career highs in points (15.4) and rebounds (10.0) in 2011–12
- Averaged at least 1.3 blocks per game from 2009–10 to 2014–15
- Set career highs in points (31) and rebounds (16) in 2014 playoffs

a line of 15.4 points and a career-best 10 boards per game. He also began blocking at least one shot per game, a pace he's improved upon since. Gortat also clicked with Steve Nash, developing the chemistry a successful big needs to have when working with a pass-first guard; and that is something he's transferred into his relationship with current point guard John Wall, one of the emerging superstars in the league. Gortat said in 2014 of that budding relationship, "I definitely taught him to slow down . . . on the pick-and-roll," something he learned from the recently retired Nash.

Last summer, he signed a massive five-year, $60 million contract with the Wizards after putting up huge numbers the season prior—13.2 points per game, 9.5 rebounds, 1.5 blocks and a .542 field goal percentage. More importantly, he provided a big body in the paint that can consistently score, defend or simply outmuscle opponents. He may not be the world's best free-throw shooter, coming in at under 70 percent, but

he more than makes up for it in intangibles. The only Polish-born player in the association, he's strong as an ox and hard to miss. He once ripped a towel in half after a foul call. He sports a Mohawk and a chinstrap beard. He has a size 15 shoe. And yet earlier this season, the Washington Post called him "the smiling soul" of the Wizards. Teammate Bradley Beal said around the same time, "He's a better person off the court."

Gortat started all 82 games for the Wizards in 2014–15, essentially duplicating his 2013–14 line while improving his field goal percentage to .566. He posted 21 points and 13 rebounds versus Pau Gasol and the Chicago Bulls in January 2015, and 14 and 14 against his former Orlando team in February. He's nearly a double-double machine and has made himself at home as the driving force up front for the Wiz. And when Gortat starts throwing his body around a little too much, he's got a backup in Nene, the veteran Brazilian who clocks in at 6-foot-11

and 250 pounds, a beast of a man who has averaged double figures in points over his long career.

With Gortat and Nene up front, and Wall and Beal anchoring the backcourt, Washington is poised to contend in a way they almost never have. But perhaps the final straw to stir the drink was "the Polish Hammer," the gregarious big from Europe who has suddenly, at 30 years old, become one of the great international stars in the NBA. A combination of genetics, the right attitude and the right team has made Gortat one of the most interesting players to hop across the pond, and of course, with that Mohawk, one of the most recognizable.

AL HORFORD 15

QUIETLY, ALMOST UNOBTRUSIVELY, Al Horford has become one of the best power forwards in the game, helping propel the Atlanta Hawks from perennial first-round knockout to one of the premier teams in the association.

Horford's quiet ascent may be because he hails from the Dominican Republic, a tiny island nation known primarily for producing baseball players. But Horford never picked up a glove. His father played pro basketball for several years, and with his son's height and interest in the game, the elder Horford moved the family to Michigan when Al was 14 years old. At the All-Star Game in 2015, which featured Horford and three of his Atlanta teammates, the power forward remarked, "I fell in love with [basketball] real quick, watching my dad play."

Horford set myriad high school records in his new home state before making the jump to college at the esteemed University of Florida. His move followed his father's footsteps, as Tito Horford went to the Sunshine State to suit up for the Miami Hurricanes in the late 1980s. The younger Horford made an immediate impact at Florida and, along with future NBA stars Corey Brewer and Joakim Noah, led the school during his sophomore year to an NCAA Final Four title against UCLA. It wouldn't be the last, as the trio tasted glory again the following year, and the center entered the NBA as a two-time national champion, something very few players can say.

Graceful even at 6-foot-10, Horford had a solid rookie year, putting up a respectable 10.1 points and 9.7 rebounds while averaging 31.4 minutes. He nearly duplicated those numbers the following year before breaking out in his third season in the NBA, with a per-game line of 14.2 points, 9.9 boards and 79 percent shooting from the

line. More impressively, he's maintained a career .541 field goal percentage over the course of his eight years in the league; the only time he's ever dipped below 50 percent from the floor was his rookie season (49.9).

Horford's an old-school center: a classic pick-and-roll big man who sets screens for guards like Jeff Teague to at-

CAREER HIGHLIGHTS

- Named an NBA All-Rookie (First Team) in 2007–08
- Named Rookie of the Month three times in 2007–08
- Has played in three All-Star Games (2010, 2011, 2015)
- Was NBA Shooting Stars champion in 2011
- Set career highs in blocks (1.5) and points (18.6) in 2013–14

A torn pectoral muscle cost Horford more than half the 2012–13 season, but in the 2014–15 campaign the Dominican essentially picked up where he left off, while also continuing to cement his role on a pass-happy offense that saw Atlanta post the second most assists per game (25.6) in the NBA.

With Horford back in the fold, teammate Kyle Korver called the power forward "the captain of our team" and "a calming presence." Maybe that's how they jumped out to a 35-8 start in 2014–15, putting together a 19-game winning streak and finishing 60-22 in the standings. Against Detroit in January, Horford scored 19 points and plucked 16 off the glass. He dropped his first career triple-double against Philadelphia three games later, recording 21 points, 10 rebounds and 10 assists during the Hawks' lengthy winning streak. Several days later he absolutely posterized Amir Johnson of the Toronto Raptors with a one-hand dunk after sidestepping another big in Jonas Valanciunas. To cap off the month, he twice posted a double-double while adding three blocks. Quite simply, his smooth combination of skill, speed and athleticism makes him one of the most well rounded power forwards in the game.

Horford finished the 2014–15 season averaging 15.2 points and 7.2 rebounds per contest. He hit 76 percent of his free-throw attempts and also chipped in a block and a steal per contest. His consistency continued in the playoffs, when in Game 5 versus the plucky Brooklyn Nets, Horford put the Hawks on his back and finished with a line of 20 points, 15 boards, 5 assists and 2 steals. In the second round against the Washington Wizards he hit a game-winning layup in Game 5. Most notably, though, his midrange jumper looked consistent and flawless while he helped the Hawks to the third round of the playoffs for the first time in 35 years.

Horford is fast becoming a household name, one of the great internationally born basketball players on the planet. And with his help, Atlanta appears to be a formidable threat to make deep playoff runs for years to come.

tack the basket or look for the open man. He's a strong presence on the back end and the leader of the Hawks on and off the court. He's also dialed in from the midrange, possessing a sweet stroke defenders need to be wary of. He's a three-time NBA All-Star and a fulcrum of the resurgent Hawks offense.

SERGE IBAKA 9

THE FIRST NBA player from the Republic of Congo, Serge Ibaka has risen to become the defensive force in the Oklahoma City Thunder's starting five. And the 6-foot-10 center—who's a three-time All-Defensive First Team selection—is only getting better.

Ibaka may be Congolese, but he's also multinational in terms of his citizenry. After cutting his teeth in the Spanish pro league, he loved the country so much he applied for citizenship. Once approved, he suited up for the Spanish national team, winning silver at the 2012 Olympics alongside the Gasol brothers.

Ibaka was selected by the Thunder (then the SuperSonics) with the 24th pick in the 2008 draft and debuted a year later as a 20-year-old in 2009–10. He saw limited action, suiting up for just over 18 minutes per game, and scored at a respectable but not remarkable rate of 6.3 points per game. His 5.4 rebounds per contest were stellar for his limited time on the floor, a strong indication of things to come. That season the Thunder managed to squeeze into the playoffs as the eighth seed, and while the veteran-laden Los Angeles Lakers eventually ousted the young team, Ibaka had time to shine. His 7-block performance in Game 2 of that series was an eye-opener for the entire league.

The following season, Ibaka started 44 games, splitting duties with incumbent Nenad Krstic, and his numbers increased accordingly, with per-game averages of 9.9

points, 7.6 boards and 2.4 blocks. With the three-headed attack of Kevin Durant, Russell Westbrook and James Harden, the Thunder went deep into the postseason, losing in the third round to the Dallas Mavericks. The run established Oklahoma as a perennial playoff contender, and the African center proved to many that he was ready for the pressure of the big stage.

His arrival as a big-time defender came in his third season, 2011–12. Ibaka led all players in total blocks (241) and blocks per game (3.7) that season while adding a midrange jumper to his offensive arsenal. In 2012–13 his well-rounded play had him leading all NBA players who attempted 300 or more shots from the midrange in field goal percentage. His former coach, Scott Brooks, called Ibaka "one of the best midrange shooters in the league," and he was right, as the center's numbers bested All-Stars Chris Paul and Marc Gasol. His growing repertoire also spoke to the Congolese player's desire to get better in all facets of the game, and he didn't sacrifice his defense either, again leading the league in total blocks and blocks per game.

But 2014–15 was a difficult season for a Thunder team with championship aspirations. Durant missed 55 games, Westbrook missed 15, Ibaka missed 18 and the Thunder missed the playoffs. Ibaka still finished third in the league in blocks per game with 2.4, and despite a dip in his typically stellar field goal percentage, his offensive numbers weren't far off pace given that Durant's absence often translated into fewer open looks for the big center. He finished the season with 14.3 points per game, 7.8 rebounds and a .836 free-throw percentage.

Oft forgotten behind the pizzazz of the Thunder's two backcourt stars, Ibaka is arguably as important to the Thunder as Durant and Westbrook. He's bucked the trend of shot-blockers being simply that; he is now as well rounded a big as they come. "At that position, there are only a few guys that can shoot that well," Westbrook says of his teammate.

Ibaka's finishing touch creates space for his guards to be creative, and it's why the Thunder, as a team, are as tough an opponent as there is in the NBA right now—no matter who is injured or where they sit in the standings. It's a testament to the hard work Ibaka has put in, bringing him from war-torn Brazzaville to the Spanish league and all the way to Oklahoma. There, night in and night out, he sets up in the paint, patiently reading the post move of an opposing player, or he runs up the court, and instead of driving to the basket, he steps back, effortlessly for a 6-foot-10 center, and hits nothing but net.

CAREER HIGHLIGHTS

- Named to NBA All-Defensive First Team three times (2011–12 to 2013–14)
- Led the NBA in block percentage in 2011–12 (9.8)
- Led the NBA in blocks twice (2011–12, 2012–13)
- Led the NBA in total blocks for four consecutive seasons (2010–11 to 2013–14)
- Won an Olympic silver medal with the Spanish men's basketball team in London in 2012

DALLAS MAVERICKS

POSITION POWER FORWARD–CENTER / **SHOOTS** RIGHT / **HEIGHT** 7'0" / **WEIGHT** 245 LB. / **DRAFTED** 1998, MILWAUKEE BUCKS, 9TH OVERALL

DIRK NOWITZKI [41]

DIRK NOWITZKI IS a freak in the best way. Few NBA big men have been blessed with his rare combination of size and skill; fewer still come from Europe. Nowitzki grew up in Germany as an anomaly among anomalies. Born into an athletic family—his mother was a basketball player and his father played handball—Nowitzki even tried soccer and tennis before focusing on the rim. The decision paid off for the 7-foot power forward from Wurzburg, who has become the best European to ever play the game.

Recently rising above fellow big Hakeem Olajuwon on the NBA's all-time career points chart, Nowitzki cracked the top 10 in 2014 and seems easily capable of climbing the ladder to sixth by the time he finally calls it quits. His point total is an impressive feat for anyone, let alone a Euro who was largely a mystery to anyone beyond the NBA's inner circle when he was drafted in 1998. Taken ninth by the Milwaukee Bucks, Nowitzki was traded on draft day to the Dallas Mavericks, where he has remained his entire career.

His rookie year was a challenging one as he adjusted to playing higher competition than in Europe. He averaged just over 20 minutes a game and collected 8.2 points and 3.4 rebounds as the Mavs finished well outside the playoffs. But an ownership change from Ross Perot Jr. to billionaire Mark Cuban altered the course of the franchise and Nowitzki's career as the

Mavs went from a thrifty league also-ran to a team that invested in success. Cuban upgraded everything: from the food the players ate and the hotels they stayed in to the arena they called home.

In Nowitzki's second season, the Mavs nearly made the playoffs and his numbers increased—17.5 points per game, 6.5

rebounds and 2.5 assists. With a winning culture instilled in Dallas, the power forward's third season was remarkable. The Mavs made the playoffs for the first time in over a decade, and Nowitzki significantly increased his output, putting up 21.8 points, 9.2 rebounds and 2.1 assists. He was finally adjusting to the bigger, faster forwards that had confounded him early on. That season "the Dunking Deutschman" also dropped more than 100 three-pointers and 100 blocks, becoming only the second NBA player at the time to do so and establishing himself as a threat to step back and knock down a deep ball, which gave him a little more room to operate. Although the Mavs bowed out in the second round to the San Antonio Spurs, the German forward impressed the league with a 42-point, 18-rebound performance in Game 5 of the series. That Mavs team also saw the emergence of another international star, Canadian Steve Nash, who arrived at the same time as Nowitzki (via trade from Phoenix), and the two formed a potent one-two punch for Dallas in the early 2000s. But in a tough conference, the two made it no further than the Western Conference finals, and Nash returned to Phoenix, where he was twice named league MVP.

Dallas eventually appeared in an NBA Finals, when Dirk powered the club forward in 2005–06, posting career-best totals of 26.6 points per game in the regular season and 27 points per playoff contest. Despite being up 2-0, over the Dwyane Wade–led Miami Heat, Dallas was torched in the next four, and Nowitzki's reputation took an undeserved hit as a choker.

Nowitzki set out to prove his detractors wrong the following year, winning the MVP award on 50.2 percent shooting and leading Dallas to a first overall regular season finish in the West. But the team came crashing down again in the postseason, becoming the first number one seed to ever lose to an eighth seed. Again, in a league where only championships matter, Nowitzki was unfairly tagged as a player who couldn't get the job done when it mattered most.

Nowitzki is one of the few players in the league who can say he's played for just one team. And he is certainly beloved in Dallas, where current Mavericks teammate Tyson Chandler called his play "timeless." The 7-foot German has dominated in the post throughout his career thanks to a difficult-to-defend step-back jumper that's been his

moneymaker during his 16 years in Texas. It was no more apparent than in 2011, when Dirk willed his way to a ring, as he and the Mavs defeated a Miami Heat team still trying to find its way after the signings of Chris Bosh and LeBron James. The win was extra sweet for Dallas, as the franchise was able to avenge its hard-to-swallow 2006 finals loss.

Mavericks owner Mark Cuban has said publicly "he will never trade Dirk." The consummate professional, adored by his teammates, Nowitzki is a once-in-a-generation star. By the time he finally hangs them up, he'll surely go down as a Hall of Famer and the best foreign basketball player the world has ever seen. Until then, take joy in watching him step back in the paint, fall away and hit nothing but net.

CAREER HIGHLIGHTS

- Named NBA Most Valuable Player for 2006–07
- Named MVP of the NBA Finals for 2010–11
- Won the NBA Three-Point Shootout in 2006
- Has played in 13 All-Star Games (2002–2012, 2014–2015)
- Averaged at least 21 points per game for 12 consecutive seasons (2000–01 to 2011–12)

SAN ANTONIO SPURS

POSITION POINT GUARD / **SHOOTS** RIGHT / **HEIGHT** 6'2" / **WEIGHT** 180 LB. / **DRAFTED** 2001, SAN ANTONIO SPURS, 28TH OVERALL

TONY PARKER [9]

FEW EUROPEANS HAVE made as big an impact on the NBA as Tony Parker has in the last decade. The sly point guard, drafted 28th overall in 2001, has become one of the great international players of all time and one of the stalwarts on a San Antonio Spurs team that's become a modern-day dynasty.

Scouted by then Spurs employee and now current Oklahoma Thunder GM Sam Presti, the Spurs took a risk with Parker, an unheralded kid from across the pond who played one pro season in France and suited up internationally in FIBA's junior tournaments. Parker, whose mother is Dutch and father American, got his start as a high schooler at INSEP, the top sports development program in Paris. Having never attended a U.S. college or played North American basketball, his first several years at the point running the Spurs' of-fense—with the likes of future Hall of Famers David Robinson and Tim Duncan—were challenging.

"It was hard the first three or four years," Parker recalled. Gregg Popovich, the Spurs' legendary coach, pushed the European to adapt to the NBA quickly, and it wasn't always pretty. "When I look back on it," Parker continued, "he made me very strong mentally."

Despite making 77 appearances his rookie year, he was still getting his sea legs in the NBA. Early knocks on Parker included questions about his physicality on the court, his lack of defensive prowess and

his lackadaisical attitude in practice. His per-game line of 9.2 points and 4.3 assists was pedestrian, especially given his nearly 30 minutes of playing time.

His second season, 2002–03, saw a surge in production (15.5 points per game) that helped propel the Spurs to the 2003

championship. Excellent shot selection and strong dribble penetration are keys to his success on the hardcourt, and it was these elements that the future star began to hone.

After reworking his shot in the 2005 off-season, Parker turned a corner. With his new release, coupled with a renewed

focus on taking two-pointers instead of three-pointers, he shot above 50 percent for the first time in his career, posting a .548 field goal percentage. That mark remains his single-season high, and his career mark of .494 illustrates his continued commitment to wise shot selection. In 2012–13, Parker put up a nifty .845 free-throw percentage. It is consistency that he's lauded for.

Yet, like the best franchise players, he saves his best performances for the playoffs. When the Spurs swept LeBron James and the Cleveland Cavaliers in 2007, Parker was unstoppable, averaging 24.5 points per game and shooting 56.8 percent from the field en route to becoming the first European player to win the playoff MVP. "I'm speechless," he said after winning the award. "I put in a lot of work to get here." Tim Duncan, the Spurs superstar, remarked: "I had no chance at the MVP. Tony carried us." It was the third championship in five years and showed just how far Parker had come, from in over his

head to hero in a manner of six seasons. The crafty 6-foot-2 guard has won four rings with the Spurs and has been named a six-time All-Star.

In 2008, Parker went off for 55 points and 10 assists in a double OT victory versus Minnesota, hitting a game-tying 20-foot jumper to send the game into the final frame. During the 2011–12 season, Parker set a career high in assists with 7.7 dimes per game to go with his 18.3 points over the course of the season. His role as ball distributor and offense runner is a huge reason San Antonio has flourished all these years; his next-level basketball IQ is perhaps his most underrated quality.

Parker may be entering the twilight of his career, but he's still making an impact on the court, averaging 14.4 points and 4.9 assists per game in 2014–15. It is certain Parker, Manu Ginobili and Duncan will go down as one of the NBA's greatest trios, and by far the greatest testament to international basketball in the history of the NBA.

CAREER HIGHLIGHTS

- Named MVP of the NBA Finals for 2006–07
- Named an NBA All-Rookie (First Team) in 2001–02
- Has played in six All-Star Games (2006–2007, 2009, 2012–2014)
- Is the all-time assists leader in San Antonio
- Is an eight-time NBA Player of the Week

Together they have been a nearly unstoppable force of nature, and despite their advancing age they can still give teams fits. Couple in their long relationship with coach Popovich, and it's clear that chemistry can mean everything to a basketball club. And although it took the point guard a few seasons to get it, that understanding has made Parker one of the best international players the world has ever seen.

TORONTO RAPTORS

POSITION CENTER / **SHOOTS** RIGHT / **HEIGHT** 7'0" / **WEIGHT** 255 LB. / **DRAFTED** 2011, TORONTO RAPTORS, 5TH OVERALL

JONAS VALANCIUNAS 17

AS FAR AS international powerhouses go in basketball, Lithuania has always had a plethora of players who have made the jump to the NBA, especially centers. Names like Arvydas Sabonis and Zydrunas Ilgauskas paved the way for budding star Jonas Valanciunas, who is fast becoming one of the NBA's best young centers.

The young European comes from solid stock: his father was an elite rower and clearly passed along some genetic material perfectly suited for athletics. By 14, Valanciunas moved to the Lithuanian capital of Vilnius to take up basketball at a higher level, and he soon competed at the U-16 European Championships as a 15-year-old. Selected fifth overall in 2011 by the Toronto Raptors, he debuted in 2012 with a solid line: 12 points and 10 rebounds in 23 minutes of action. Although he never jumped to the United States for college, the center hustled in Lithuania and briefly in the Euroleague before arriving in Canada, winning several gold medals at the FIBA tournament for his home country. The scouting report on Valanciunas was that he was a determined youngster with a high compete level and a slick touch on the ball who was effective under the rim in catch-and-finish situations. That translated to ample time in a starting role for the then-lowly Raptors, as he registered 8.9 points per game, 6 boards and 1.3 blocks after starting 57 games as an NBA rookie.

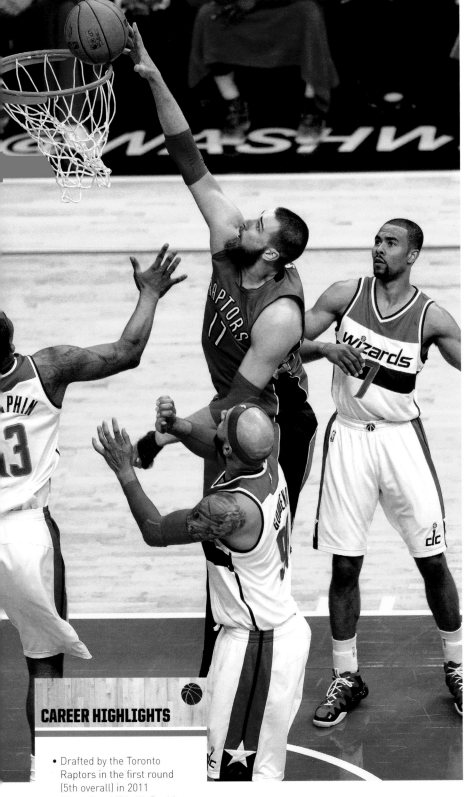

and regularly backs downs opponents, especially when his new brawn gives him a size advantage. One night in March, he deftly dropped a baby hook on legendary Tim Duncan. On other nights, he's running the screen and roll to perfection and barging his way to the basket. Is he a work in progress? Sure. But he's nearly an 80 percent free-throw shooter, still averaging just over 25 minutes per game as coach Dwane Casey eases the big fella into important stretches late in the fourth quarter.

He's come up huge in several games, including his 18-point, 12-rebound and 4-block performance in December 2014 versus the Denver Nuggets. To start 2015, the Lithuanian put up 31 and 12 versus the Detroit Pistons in January. In the spring, he kept it up, registering 26 and 10 against Cleveland in March when he went toe-to-toe with Timofey Mozgov, a fellow international baller and giant of a man who hails from nearby Russia. In the month of January alone, Valanciunas' field goal percentage was 61 percent, and he shot 87 percent from the line. His coach praised his "skill, strength and willingness to work." Casey went on to laud how "coachable" the 22-year-old Lithuanian is for the Raptors, especially in relation to those shrinking late-game minutes the center isn't quite ready for. Read between the lines and you get the idea the Lithuanian is highly focused, patient with the growing process and looking to improve in all facets of the game.

Like a lot of young players, he still has a lot to learn on the defensive end, but with his work ethic, Valanciunas should be poised in several years to be one of the best bigs in the league alongside LaMarcus Aldridge and DeMarcus Cousins. The Raptors are hoping he evolves into a dependable double-double man, and the dream is that he consistently nets 20 points and 10 rebounds per game. If Valanciunas can accomplish that, the Raptors have a star in the making, and he could quite easily surpass his forebears from his home country as one of the great basketball players to ever emerge from Lithuania.

CAREER HIGHLIGHTS

- Drafted by the Toronto Raptors in the first round (5th overall) in 2011
- Named an NBA All-Rookie (Second Team) in 2012–13
- Named FIBA World Under-19 Championship MVP (2011)
- Named Lithuanian Player of the Year three times (2011, 2012, 2014)
- Finished second in the NBA with a .572 field goal percentage in 2014–15

Just completing his third year in the league in 2014–15, Valanciunas has emerged as a bona fide weapon for the now-surging Raptors, who made the playoffs for a second straight year after a long period of watching from the outside in. Now at 7 feet tall and 255 pounds, he's a force in the paint, with nifty post moves that belie his size. Despite adding size since his rookie season, he's also improved his footwork

ORLANDO MAGIC

POSITION CENTER / **SHOOTS** RIGHT / **HEIGHT** 7'0" / **WEIGHT** 260 LB. / **DRAFTED** 2011, PHILADELPHIA 76ERS, 16TH OVERALL

NIK VUCEVIC [9]

FROM THE TINY country of Montenegro hails a giant. The son of Yugoslavian basketball players, Nik Vucevic followed in their footsteps, eventually landing in the United States with a thud, all 7 feet of him. He's become a quiet, unheralded star who just might be the most under-the-radar center in the NBA today.

He spent three years with the University of Southern California Trojans after moving to the States and was drafted 16th overall in 2011 by the Philadelphia 76ers. But his stock truly rose after the draft when he spent time during the 2011 NBA lockout playing in Europe. Scouts marveled at his length, rebounding and creative scoring.

In his final year at USC, Vucevic managed 17.1 points per game and 10.3 off the boards before declaring for the draft following his junior year of college. He toiled for one year with the lowly Philadelphia franchise before a four-team, 12-player trade sent the European to the Orlando Magic, where he established himself as one of young rising big men in the NBA today.

When you're swapped in a deal that involves Dwight Howard, Andrew Bynum and Andre Iguodala, there's a lot to live up to. The weight was no problem for Vucevic. In January 2015, LA Clippers coach Doc Rivers called Vucevic "the best player in the league that nobody knows." Boston Celtics coach Brad Stevens went further, suggesting, "he may very well be an All-Star in the East at some point."

At 7 feet tall and 260 pounds, he's a quiet goliath, posting mammoth numbers in his fourth NBA season: 19.3 points a game, second highest among centers, and 10.5 boards, which ranked him fifth. His current coach describes his skill set as such: "Ability to shoot the basketball, ability to handle the ball in the post." He may not be a block-happy center on defense, but he makes up for that at the other end, using both hands to make sly moves in the post, or popping off the pick and roll and making his way to the basket, preferring "short rolls, the half-hook or half-floater," as he put it midway through 2014–15. Plus, he has improved every year—in year one with Philadelphia, he started just 15 games, played in 51 and averaged just 5.5 points and 4.8 boards. At the end of year three with Orlando, Vucevic posted 14.2 points per game and 11.2 rebounds, and he put up a field goal percentage above .500. His emphatic 24 points and 23 boards versus Charlotte late in the 2013–14 season signaled the best is yet to come.

In 2014–15, "Vooch" was a double-double threat every night on the floor. Against his former team before Christmas, he went off for 19 and 17. He posted back-to-back 30-point games several weeks later. His best month of the season came in February: 36.2 minutes a game, with 22.2 points and 11.5 off the glass. He capped off his best NBA season yet with a 37-point, 17-rebound performance against the lowly Minnesota Timberwolves on 18-of-25 shooting. His recent signing of a four-year, $53 million deal with the Magic means Orlando fans need not worry about the center of the future. Vucevic played the second-most minutes for centers in the NBA and amassed 45 double-doubles, fourth highest in the league behind DeAndre Jordan, DeMarcus Cousins and Andre Drummond. He's enjoyed his time so much in Florida that near the end of the season, he claimed he wanted to be a member of the Magic for life.

Alongside Chicago Bulls rookie Nikola Mirotic and Minnesota Timberwolves big man Nikola Pekovic, the three—hailing from a country of just 650,000—are making a name for Montenegrin basketball. But it's Vucevic who could transform to a superstar. In Orlando he's posting All-Star-type numbers for a rebuilding team. If he keeps it up, expect to see the big man from Montenegro lead the Magic back to the playoffs, following another big who made a name for himself in Orlando, Hall of Famer Shaquille O'Neal.

CAREER HIGHLIGHTS

- Drafted by the Philadelphia 76ers in the first round (16th overall) in 2011
- Set a career high in points (37) in 2014–2015
- Finished second in two-point field goals (629) in 2014–2015
- Finished second in rebounding (11.9) in 2012–13 and sixth in rebounding (10.9) in 2014–2015
- Holds the Orlando Magic record for rebounds in one game (29)

THE DUNK CONTEST

ON FEBRUARY 9TH, 1991, it's fair to say few inside the Charlotte Coliseum had heard of a 6-foot shooting guard named Dee Brown. In the past, winners of the NBA Slam Dunk Contest—stars such as Dominique Wilkins, Michael Jordan and Spud Webb, who would define their early careers with the exposure at the annual All-Star Game— were already known to the masses. Not so for the Celtics rookie. When the unknown shooting guard leaned down, pumped up his Reebok shoes and leapt toward the basket with one arm draped over his eyes, he entered NBA lore, winning the 1991 dunk contest with the now-famous no-look dunk. Immediately immortalized thereafter on posters and in magazines, the jam heard 'round the world prompted Magic Johnson to say on air that February night: "Everybody at home, don't try that. That is unbelievable." The dunk is so iconic that Brown's daughter, now a college basketball player

Zach LaVine, the 2015 dunk champ, slams under the spotlight during the 2015 competition.

Dee Brown drapes his arm over his eyes for a no-look jam at the 1991 Slam Dunk Contest. The creative dunk won Brown the contest and made him an instant sensation.

herself, cannot escape questions about her father's moment in the spotlight nearly 25 years ago.

More so than Jordan's stretch slam from the foul line, Wilkins' windmill or Vince Carter's between the legs, Brown's no-looker sent the dunk contest to another stratosphere and etched his name on the lips of young fans for years down the road. A vital change had occurred: no longer was the evening designed for a select group of well-known individuals. No longer was it a superstar's athleticism shining through. Dee Brown was just a kid, an everyman, wearing second-tier shoes and flashing a Gumby flattop haircut. His creative, organic flair began an era at the All-Star Game that encouraged out-of-box thinking, something that would become a trademark for the next generation of NBA players for years to come.

IN THE (NEAR) BEGINNING

The name Larry Nance likely conjures up a whole lot of . . . diddly squat. But in 1984, Nance was named the winner of the first NBA Slam Dunk Contest, edging out the legendary Julius Erving for the $10,000 prize. The contestants that year in Denver were a ragtag group—legends like Erving, unheralded middle-of-the-road 80s NBA stars like Darrell Griffith and Michael Cooper, and a few off-the-map rookies. It was a motley crew to say the least.

As for marquee stars, Dr. J was already a household name inside and outside the league, nearing the end of his career. He gained early fame for his history-altering dunk from the free-throw line in 1976 at the ABA All-Star Game, the first dunk contest of its kind, also held in Denver, and he was widely known around the NBA for spectacular in-game slams. Atlanta Hawks stud Dominique Wilkins—drafted third overall in the 1982 draft—was still young but already making a name for himself as a power-slamming specialist known as "the Human Highlight Film." Trail Blazers guard Clyde "the Glide" Drexler may have been a first-year player and unknown outside the Portland area, but anyone who followed his career in college knew he was a product of "Phi Slama Jama,"

the Houston squad that defined their team around lob plays and high-flying dunks. (To all those Clippers fans, that's the original Lob City.) Then there was all 7-foot-4 of Ralph Sampson, the former rookie of the year and the tallest player in the competition. The judges were equally offbeat and included a Colorado congresswoman and a New York Mets catcher.

Dr. J was the man to beat of course, and in 2014, Darrell Griffith (whose nickname was Dr. Dunkenstein) said: "[Erving] still had hops. He had them bear claw hands. He could grab the ball like it was an orange." Fan participation included scribbling numbers on handmade cards to rate dunks, something that gained in popularity as time went on, becoming a staple in the stands and at the judges table as the contest progressed. And although Nance may have been proclaimed the winner by points—and bought a Camaro with his

Dr. J is in full flight at the first-ever professional slam dunk competition, which took place at the 1976 ABA All-Star Game. Dr. J won the competition with this jam that started from the free-throw line.

winnings—the moment of the night belonged to Erving when he revisited his '76 ABA slam by running the length of the floor, leaping from behind the charity stripe once again and scoring the first perfect score of the night. The crowd went wild. "The whole show was just a buildup for Dr. J," contestant Michael Cooper said years later. "You could feel the electricity in the gym."

Jordan would re-create Dr. J's dunk several years later in 1988—it too immortalized poster form, perhaps even one that Dee Brown had in his room. Posters were currency in the pre-Internet NBA, street cred for the athletically inclined teenager, a way to show off one's allegiance to a team or a newfound hero who could do amazing things with a basketball. Those posters of high-flying heroes showing off their moves in the dunk contest populated the bedrooms of basketball fans years before kids traded in still images for YouTube videos.

Although the modern-day dunk competition may have morphed into more spectacle than contest—with cool sneakers and trick dunks the norm—there's something still exciting about seeing one

man on the court, seconds before he leaps in the air, trying something no one has ever dared attempt. It is the moment where "what if?" becomes reality.

THE LAST GREAT DUNK

The 1990s following Dee Brown's signature slam was a largely forgettable era of dunking, and by the time Brent Barry—AKA the only white guy to ever win the Slam Dunk Contest—was declared the winner in 1996, times had truly changed. The NBA shelved the contest for several years in a bid to regroup, and then along came Vince Carter.

The North Carolina product was a second-year player for the Toronto Raptors in 2000, the year the dunk contest ticked upward once again. That season, the fifth overall pick from the 1998 draft averaged a career-high 25.7 points per game, leading the young Raps into the playoffs for the first time in franchise history. Carter was a throwback to the old dunkers—a fluid mix of creativity, raw power and ingenuity that immediately launched him into the mix of the greatest to ever slam. His between-the-legs midair jam to claim the title vaulted him to the top of the dunking charts. Up until 2014–15, when youngster Zach LaVine wowed the crowd, many casual fans, and LaVine himself, would say Carter was the last great dunker thanks to a plethora of moves that included a 360 windmill, an elbow in the rim, or the aforementioned between-the-legs dunk. What's undeniable is that night in DC has been etched in NBA lore and is still dubbed "the last great dunk contest."

With the passage of time and Carter now a 37-year-old veteran playing out his career in Memphis, many have looked back on what that dunk symbolized for the entire country of Canada. He was quickly named "Air Canada," and "Vinsanity" arrived full force north of the border. It was a marketer's dream, much the same as when Reebok captured the zeitgeist of Dee Brown. The Raptors were desperately seeking legitimacy after a series of losing seasons to begin their tenure. Carter provided that, and if not for a game-ending clanker in the seventh contest of the Raptors' 2001 second-round playoff series versus the Allen Iverson–led Philadelphia 76ers, Toronto may have done some damage in the Eastern Conference that year.

What no one could have predicted was that a young generation of Canadian basketball fans would gravitate to Carter like moths to a flame. Soon they would be attempting Carter's awe-inspiring slams when they got older. In late 2014, Carter was honored during the first quarter of a Grizzlies–Raptors game. He looked back on his time in Toronto and the impact it had on the fans. "All of a sudden, after that first playoff win . . . everybody wanted to pick up a basketball. It was fantastic," he said. Among those fans: a seven-year-old Nik Stauskas, a Mississauga native and now a Sacramento King, and a five-year-old Andrew Wiggins, 2014–15 Rookie of the Year and the heir apparent to the Carter legend. Carter's own hero was Dr. J, and although the doctor may have inspired a legion of dunk enthusiasts, he didn't impact an entire nation like Carter.

IN THE BEGINNING

The origins of dunking date back to the early part of the 20th century. A *New York Times* writer described Joe Fortenberry, the captain of the 1936 U.S. men's basketball team, as "pitch[ing] the ball downward into the hoop, much like a cafeteria customer dunking a roll in coffee." Although this may have popularized the term nationally, *dunk* was in fact used to describe the play of stuffing the ball in the hoop in several other smaller newspapers prior to the *Times* during the early part of the 1930s. (Los Angeles Lakers play-by-play announcer Chick Hearn, who voiced the team for 42 years

Michael Jordan pays homage to Dr. J and his legendary 1976 charity-stripe slam with his own dunk from the stripe at the 1988 Slam Dunk Contest.

before his death in 2002, is widely acknowledged as creating the saying "slam dunk" with specificity to Wilt Chamberlain.) For years following, many in the game, from general managers to coaches, tried to eliminate dunking, or at the very least, raise the rim to 12 feet to thwart the practice. An underlying subtext, especially by the 1950s and 1960s, was more than likely the increasing number of African-American players in the game, and their ability to dunk more often than their white counterparts. Beyond any racial subtext, the prevailing opinion was that as players were getting taller, dunking was changing the game, and in 1940, one American wrote: "Many people claim that there is no premium on accuracy. That instead of beautiful shooting, slap happy basketball has resulted with wild throwing from every possible angle calculated to get the ball into range of the backboards where the skyscraper boys bat it down for two points."

The three-point line that emerged in the NBA in 1979, basketball's version of a home run, was a direct response to a league that had changed, especially with the likes of massive centers skilled in the art of slamming, including Kareem Abdul-Jabbar, Bill Russell and Chamberlain. The NCAA even banned dunking for nearly a decade following Abdul-Jabbar's dominance at UCLA in the 60s, when he won three straight national championships, compiling a record of 88-2. Adding a three-point line—thanks to pressure and ingenuity from ABA commish George Mikan in 1967—lengthened the game, creating a faster, more up-tempo pace that took the focus away from the paint and allowed guards to flourish. What we see today is a guard-heavy game that's focused on hitting an open man for three in transition, or moving the ball around the perimeter to find an open shot, rather than feeding a big man like Abdul-Jabbar in the paint.

MODERN-DAY DUNKS

But it's not raining threes for everyone. Just ask Zach LaVine. In 2015, a much-needed uplift occurred in the dunking department thanks to the jaw-dropping performance of the 19-year-old Minnesota Timberwolves shooting guard. In an age where posters are obsolete and six-second Vines appear mere moments after a live play, the Timberwolves' rising star did not disappoint. He confidently donned a No. 23 Michael Jordan jersey and mimicked a Space Jam dunk, going through the legs and up for a reverse one-hander. It was sick. He flipped the ball in the air again on the second attempt and then went around his own back in midair, perhaps the most innovative of his four dunks. LaVine had the select group of NBA All-Stars flying out of their seats in amazement. For a contest that desperately needed a shot in the arm after several lackluster years— Dr. J had said the year prior, "You might never get back to the day when you've got the two best players in the league . . . facing off, like you did in the heyday"—LaVine delivered, at least in terms of a solo effort. Was it on par with Carter, Erving, Wilkins and MJ? Quite possibly. LaVine has called Carter "the best dunker of all time." But now, at the very least, the kid deserves to be mentioned with the greats, particularly since the contest itself has suffered some growing pains throughout the last decade.

What was it exactly about LaVine's performance that stood out from, say, his competitor Victor Oladipo? That "wow" factor. All great dunkers have it. A sense of showmanship, talent and raw power all wrapped into one. Sure, Dwight Howard's Superman cape in 2008 was fun, but was it awe-inspiring? Hardly. Steve Nash's

Two-time dunk champion Dominique Wilkins, known for his aggressive rim-shaking slams, pounds this ball down at the 1988 Slam Dunk Contest.

soccer header to Amar'e Stoudemire was crafty and clever, but come on. Gerald Green blowing out a candle in 2007 on a cupcake was kind of *hard*? Was it really that cool when 5-foot-9 Nate Robinson launched himself over former winner Spud Webb? Sure, for a half-second and for the sheer fact he could elevate that high. Robinson—a three-time dunk contest champ, who also jumped over the aforementioned Howard—undoubtedly wowed the crowd. But something beyond simple elevation is needed to capture the imagination of the fans and become legendary. (Arguably, Webb's two-handed reverse in 1986, after lobbing the ball in the air 10-plus feet, was purer in form and 20 years earlier. Plus, he was only 5-foot-7, and watching Webb spring from an average man's height to the rim is pure theater.)

Like Webb's gravity-defying leap, the greatest dunks in the history of the contest have always been simple in concept, difficult in execution, pure in power. Take Wilkins, "the Human Highlight Film," two-time winner of the dunk contest, one in 1985, another in

Zach LaVine pays homage to both Michael Jordan and Vince Carter with his Toon Squad through-the-legs slam that helped him win the 2015 title.

1990. In '85, up against his longtime dunking rival, Jordan, Wilkins' windmill dunk helped secure his status as an elite player and put the Hawks on the map. Forever in the shadow of the Bulls star—he consistently finished second in league scoring to MJ—that was one night where Wilkins came out on top. In 2015, Wilkins described his own style as bringing an element of "flare and power to the dunk contest." The Hawks star certainly did that in '85.

Although Jordan would go on to defeat Wilkins famously in 1988 by launching himself from (almost) the charity stripe à la Dr. J, because the All-Star weekend occurred in Chicago, many, including Wilkins, believed MJ's perfect score for his final dunk was blatant home favoritism. Wilkins, in 2014, even acknowledged in an interview that the famously competitive Jordan once told him: "You probably won. You know it, I know it. But we're in Chicago. What can I tell you?" Wilkins went on to say that of the five dunk contests he participated in, he "won four, but got credit for two." All said, it was a natural rivalry from two great competitors of the game, and something rarely seen in the modern era, particularly as many competitors now are rookies or up-and-coming stars in the league without much history. Who knows—maybe the Oladipo–LaVine rivalry is just beginning.

SO WHERE DO we go from here? LaVine may have changed the game going forward, incorporating old-style dunks with a modern twist and making us all forget about the recent exploits of Robinson and Howard. In a clip that aired before the 2015 contest, a young LaVine discussed his early obsession with watching old dunk contests, particularly Jordan, something Carter admitted to doing as well. It showed, and maybe that's the way to a new era—look to the past. Kids need to be inspired by individuals, not spoon-fed by the league, and the NBA has done an excellent job of identifying superstars, or dunking artists like LaVine, and marketing them to fans. (Perhaps that's why NBA superstars have 10 times more Twitter followers than baseball players.)

Moving forward, the contest will likely eschew a gimmicky approach for a pure, no-holds-barred one that feels more like something that would happen organically on the playground. While Dr. J's 1976 free-throw dunk looks relatively pedestrian to modern-day jammers, watching him palm the ball, back up and run the length of the court, and leap from the line was a sight to behold back then; it was pure spectacle, akin to something Evel Knievel might have pulled off. The thrill of the improbable is where the dunk contest should reside. When Dee Brown pumped up his Reeboks, he set the stage, and from there he simply leaned down, took off and covered his eyes while the world held its breath.

DAMIAN LILLARD

POSITION POWER FORWARD–CENTER / **SHOOTS** RIGHT / **HEIGHT** 6'11" / **WEIGHT** 240 LB. / **DRAFTED** 2006, CHICAGO BULLS, 2ND OVERALL

LAMARCUS ALDRIDGE 12

LAMARCUS ALDRIDGE PREVIOUSLY carried the Portland Trail Blazers on his broad shoulders for nine seasons, saving his best for the 2014–15 campaign. But entering his prime years, the 6-foot-11 center elected to join the San Antonio Spurs as a free agent. With San Antonio's aging trio of Tim Duncan, Tony Parker and Manu Ginobili coming back for one more try at a championship, Aldridge will be a key cog in extending the legacy of the Spurs.

Born July 19, 1985, in Dallas, Aldridge was a longtime work in progress. Before starring at the University of Texas for two years and leapfrogging to the NBA, he was a skinny 6-foot-7 eighth grader with a limited arsenal and a weak hook shot. But a similarly sized older brother and an inspirational coach coaxed Aldridge to improve and not be discouraged. By his senior year in high school the lessons and hard work paid off, and he averaged 30 points and 14 rebounds per game. Once at Texas, Aldridge helped his alma mater reach the Elite Eight. His coach there said he'd "never had a player work harder to get better."

Selected second overall in the 2006 draft by the Chicago Bulls, he was instantly traded to Portland, becoming the fulcrum of a Trail Blazers team in search of a new identity after a long stretch missing the playoffs. In Portland he was able to showcase all of his many talents. His midrange jumper for a nearly seven-footer is almost unbeatable, and he's ruthlessly efficient from the normally difficult-to-hit-from distance. Alongside tenacious point guard Damian Lillard, another emerging star in the NBA, the duo formed a one-two tandem that was one of the best in the league. Aldridge has been praised for a strong basketball IQ and his commitment to hard work and fitness. The latter has helped him rebound from early career adversity that saw him contend with numerous niggling injuries and the diagnosis of a heart condition that required him to take considerable time away from the court. But the work he put in has allowed him to find the top of his game. In 2014–15 he finished eighth in the league in defensive rebounds and 10th in total rebounds per game (all despite injuring his thumb in late January). Rather than elect to undergo surgery for the injury, Aldridge played through the pain, a testament to his toughness and how much he wants to win.

His 23.4 points per game in 2014–15 set a career high, as did his free-throw percentage of .845. And following the thumb injury? He went back-to-back with 37 and 38 points versus top Eastern Conference foes Cleveland and Atlanta, adding 11 boards in each game and even dropping a pair of threes in each contest.

During one game in the 2013–14 season, Aldridge hauled down 25 boards to go along with 31 points, a phenomenal display that set a career best in rebounds. In the 2014 playoffs, he showed just how far he'd come, putting up dominant numbers in the first two games of Portland's series against Dwight Howard and the Houston Rockets, and on the road to boot. His first was a statement 46-point and 18-rebound game. It matched his career high for points in any contest and eclipsed his own previous playoff scoring record while also demolishing Portland's franchise mark.

"I want to try and break every record I can," he said following the game.

In his Game 2 sequel he repped 43 and 8. He wouldn't fare as well against future Hall of Famer Tim Duncan in the next round of the 2013–14 playoffs—his numbers dropped and the Blazers were ousted.

Still, the four-time All-Star has established

himself as one of the most unstoppable forwards in the game, a threat from anywhere on the court. His foot speed and ball skills are a nightmare for a man who matches him in size, and his 89-inch wingspan is an absolute disaster of a matchup for an undersized player. Bringing his talents back to Texas, the Spurs get a player that fits their system perfectly. He can pass the ball and he is terrific in the post—musts for San Antonio bigs. With Aldridge in the fold, don't be surprised to see the Black and Silver vying for another title.

CAREER HIGHLIGHTS

- Named an NBA All-Rookie (First Team) in 2006–07
- Has played in four All-Star Games (2012–2015)
- Set a career high in points (46) in 2013–14
- Is the Portland Trail Blazers' all-time rebounds leader
- Is an eight-time NBA Player of the Week

MEMPHIS GRIZZLIES

POSITION POINT GUARD / **SHOOTS** LEFT / **HEIGHT** 6'1" / **WEIGHT** 175 LB. / **DRAFTED** 2007, MEMPHIS GRIZZLIES, 4TH OVERALL

MIKE CONLEY 11

AT 6-FOOT-1 AND 175 pounds, Mike Conley isn't the biggest point guard in the league. And despite his name being absent from conversations about the best players at the position, he's quickly become the fulcrum of a resurgent Memphis Grizzlies team that's now challenging for league supremacy. Make no mistake: Mike Conley has slowly matured into one of the most consistent difference makers in the NBA today.

Conley comes from athletic pedigree— his father, Mike Conley Sr., won gold at the 1992 Olympics in triple jump, and his uncle played linebacker for the Pittsburgh Steelers.

Mike starred at Ohio State as a point guard for one season for the Buckeyes alongside future number one pick Greg Oden. The duo led the school to the 2007 NCAA final, where they lost to a powerhouse Florida team. Conley was drafted fourth overall by the Memphis Grizzlies in 2007. But before making the jump to Ohio and then the NBA, Oden and Conley were a force to be reckoned with, destroying the high school basketball scene in Indiana while amassing a 103-7 record with Lawrence North High School in Indianapolis. The duo led the Hoosier state to three state championships during their epic run.

When Ohio State coach Thad Matta recruited the two stars together, he said that at the time people laughed at him because he thought Conley was "the best

point guard in the country," despite the fact that "he played with Greg." Matta, of course, is having the last laugh now (though not so much for Oden, who has been hampered by injuries and has never amounted to anything resembling a number one pick).

Conley, on the other hand, has been durable and effective, running the offense for the Grizz over the last eight years. In 2013–14 he posted a career-high 17.2 points per game in addition to 6 assists. The court general has maintained a free-throw percentage of more than 80 percent and shot 37.5 percent from behind the arc his entire NBA career. He may not lead the Grizzlies in any one category, but his presence on the court and what he means to his team aren't found on the score sheet. One of his first coaches in the league, Johnny Davis, commented in early 2015 that Conley was "as important to the success of the Grizzlies as Zach Randolph and Marc Gasol. He has evolved into one of the better point guards in the league."

It's been slow and steady progress, however. He started just 46 games his rookie year. By year two, he clocked in at 60, but his numbers were average (10.9 points per game, 4.3

assists—hardly bulletin board material for the fourth overall pick), and he was sharing time in an untenable situation with future All-Star Kyle Lowry, who'd been drafted one year ahead of Conley. Lowry was eventually traded in 2009 to Houston, and Conley took over the Grizzlies' point guard position for good.

He plays primarily left-handed—despite actually being right-handed—but uses his right to drain his money shot, a short-range floater that he's been good for at more than 50 percent in recent years.

Perhaps his most admirable, unquantifiable quality is his ability to get guys going. Conley is a whiz at noticing when Randolph or Gasol needs the ball—"it's almost like you have a clock in your head," he once said—or knowing when he needs to slash toward the hoop to give the team an energy boost. He helped take the team to the Western Conference finals in 2012, which is the farthest the franchise has gone in its history.

The 2014–15 playoffs were tough on the undersized guard. Already playing with a wonky ankle, he suffered a facial fracture that required surgery at the end of the Grizzlies' first-round victory over the

CAREER HIGHLIGHTS

- Won the NBA Sportsmanship Award in 2013–14
- Named to NBA All-Defensive Second Team in 2012–13
- Finished first in the NBA in steals (174) in 2012–13
- Set a career high in points (36) in 2014–15
- Set a career-high in points per game (17.2) in 2013–14

Portland Trail Blazers. Conley gamely came back in the second round wearing a face mask versus the Golden State Warriors and sparked the Grizz to victory in Game 2 on the road—the Warriors' first loss in Oakland in 22 games dating back to the regular season. Conley's 22 points on 8-of-10 shooting underscore the emotional impact he brought to the arena that night, but it wasn't enough, and the Grizzlies' season ended at the hands of Golden State.

Conley's been labeled both an under-achiever and underrated, but it's about time both tags are shed in favor of what he actually is: the key cog to the offense of one of the best teams in the NBA—and one of the NBA's brightest stars.

POSITION CENTER / SHOOTS RIGHT / HEIGHT 6'11" / WEIGHT 270 LB. / DRAFTED 2010, SACRAMENTO KINGS, 5TH OVERALL

DEMARCUS COUSINS 15

WHEN YOU'RE 6-FOOT-6 in eighth grade, certain things seem likely. For instance, if you have a single athletic bone in your body, and you don't mind hitting people, chances are you'll find yourself on a football field.

That is exactly where DeMarcus Cousins found himself as a youth. Just as likely was that Cousins would be a shoo-in to rule the basketball court. Yet, at 14 he'd never really played. Destiny, however, has a way

of carving a path. After a chance encounter with an AAU recruiter, who thought the eighth grader was a high school senior, Cousins got his basketball start. The following year, he dominated older, bigger boys as a high school freshman, averaging 26 points, 15 rebounds and 10 assists per game with a ridiculous .700 shooting percentage. His one season of stellar play landed him on the national radar.

Born in Mobile, Alabama, Cousins flourished on the hardwood, dazzling scouts with the hands of a guard and the size of a forward. But despite a gregarious, engaging personality outside of the gym, Cousins was plagued by a reputation as a hothead on the court. He carried the stigma into college, no thanks to a suspension during high school for shoving a teacher after an argument.

Cousins spent just one year at Kentucky before jumping to the association. A fan favorite there despite playing just over 20 minutes per game, he still managed 15 points and 10 rebounds per contest. His coach, John Calipari, said Cousins was "one of the most talented big men I've ever had." Calipari went on to cite Cousins' ball-handling skills and his "mean streak" as positives for the prospect.

Before the 2010 NBA Draft—where Cousins would go fifth overall to Sacramento—the center played 1-on-1 with Kevin Durant, and despite getting crossed up, he returned the favor to the

Case in point: in the third game of the 2014–15 season, he put up 34 points and 18 rebounds against Blake Griffin and the LA Clippers, a statement game considering Griffin won Rookie of the Year in Cousins' inaugural campaign. Versus Minnesota in November, Cousins had 31 points and 18 rebounds, making 9 of 10 free throws. He went 29 and 14 the following month versus the LA Lakers, with 3 blocks to boot. And in January against Cleveland, Cousins notched 26 points, 13 rebounds, 5 dimes, 4 steals and 3 blocks. Nights like that, when he's unstoppable in all facets, are what Kings fans salivate over.

Cousins' banner year wasn't without its growing pains. His first several years in the NBA were marred by his temper and technical fouls. In 2012–13, he led the NBA with 17 Ts and tied with Griffin and Durant for the league lead the following season. Many wondered if his immense talent was being wasted because of a poor attitude. But it seemed Cousins might just be misunderstood, or that he needed a few years to throw the shackles off past transgressions—three months into the 2014–15 season, he'd racked up only two technicals.

He couldn't stay true to his preseason promise of five Ts or fewer, however. By season's end he was once again one of the NBA's worst aggressors, racking up 14 Ts for third most in the league. But maybe Cousins' foul trouble isn't that big a deal. People don't waste a lot of breath talking about Russell Westbrook's penchant for getting T'd up. He led the NBA in 2014–15 and has often been one of the league's worst offenders. The lack of emphasis on his foul trouble seems a double standard—and perhaps linked more to Cousins' position and reputation than anything else.

Cousins is only 24, barely on the precipice of his prime, so the sky's the limit for his individual success. With his not-so-private disputes with coach George Karl making waves, the big may not last in Sacramento. But one thing is certain: whatever team Cousins plays for is better off with him than without.

CAREER HIGHLIGHTS

- Named an NBA All-Rookie (First Team) in 2010–11
- Played in the 2015 NBA All-Star Game
- Led the NBA in offensive rebounds in 2011–12 (265)
- Led the NBA in defensive rebound percentage in 2013–14 (30.5)
- Has finished in the top 10 for four consecutive years in rebounds per game (2011–12 to 2014–15)

former MVP, which did not go unnoticed by the Oklahoma City star. In his rookie year Cousins turned heads with his skill set, and he put up respectable numbers: 14.1 points per game and 8.6 rebounds. The following year, despite turmoil with coach Paul Westphal, Cousins' stats improved in all facets, including steals and blocks. But he wasn't living up to his potential, and the Kings continued to be awful. (Their last winning season was 2005–06.)

At 6-foot-11 and 270 pounds, "Boogie" is one of the best bigs in the NBA.

NEW ORLEANS PELICANS

POSITION POWER FORWARD–CENTER / **SHOOTS** RIGHT / **HEIGHT** 6'10" / **WEIGHT** 220 LB. / **DRAFTED** 2012, NEW ORLEANS HORNETS, 1ST OVERALL

ANTHONY DAVIS 23

THERE'S A NEW superstar emerging in the NBA. He's tall, he's long and he sports the league's most recognizable unibrow. At 6-foot-10 and 220 pounds, Anthony Davis is fast becoming the most talked about young forward in the league. If he keeps it up, we may be watching a future MVP at work.

Born in 1993, Davis is part of a new youth movement, and at just 21, he appears to be taking his role seriously. The Chicago kid jumped from high school to the University of Kentucky, where he led the Wildcats to a national championship as a freshman in 2012 over the Kansas Jayhawks. Davis, who routinely set records for blocked shots (including most in one NCAA season), was named MVP of that game after recording 6 points, 16 rebounds, 5 assists, 6 blocks and 3 steals. Former U of K coach Tubby Smith said after the game, "He may be the best player to [ever] play at Kentucky."

His inclusion as a teenager on the 2012 U.S. men's Olympic team signaled he deserved to be mentioned among the elite, and he didn't disappoint in London. At the time, LeBron James said that Davis reminded him of four-time NBA blocks leader Marcus Camby. Kobe Bryant resolved to mentor the 19-year-old after seeing him finish alley-oops from Kevin Durant and Chris Paul. His length, defensive awareness and energy impressed the group of future Hall of Famers. It was a coming-out party for the first overall pick.

In his first full season playing for the New Orleans Hornets (2012–13), Davis played 64 games, averaging 13.5 points per game, 8.2 rebounds and 1.8 blocks despite several injury scares, including a concussion and a sprained knee. He managed to impress league-wide, posting 28 points and 11 rebounds versus Milwaukee early in the season, and consistently began dropping double-doubles in the second half, including back-to-back games in both January and February. "Fear the Brow" became a household phrase, and he punctuated his first campaign with two nasty games against Memphis, finishing with 20 points and 18 rebounds in early March, and two weeks later with 18 and 15 on 8-of-14 shooting. But the Hornets finished a measly 22-55 that season and missed the playoffs.

The following year the team name changed to the Pelicans, and it proved positive. Davis clearly focused on the little things that off-season, and he saw his totals increase. He nearly doubled his trips to the line and increased his free-throw percentage to .791—impressive for a big man. He also blocked one more shot per game throughout the entire season, for an average of nearly three swats per contest. He finished with 20.8 points per game (an increase of nearly 7 points), 10 rebounds and 2.8 blocks in 67 games, but the Pelicans still finished 34-48, good for 12th in the Western Conference but not good enough for the postseason.

His 2014–15 NBA campaign got off to a blistering start. He dropped an opening night for the ages: 26 points, 17 rebounds, 9 blocks, 3 steals and 2 assists—results not seen since the likes of another big man, Hakeem Olajuwon. Davis scored 25 points on 12-of-16 shooting against the porous LA Lakers defense early in November (and added 5 blocks), and he continually drove defenses mad with his ruthless combo of size and touch. At the end of January, he was on pace for the greatest player efficiency rating (PER) in the history of the NBA. He finished with a mark of 30.81. The only two players since 1973–74 (when the NBA began tracking individual turnovers) to have posted higher ratings? Michael Jordan and LeBron James. Pretty heady company.

If he's not making a deft post move, Davis is hitting nothing but net from 15 feet out. He can dribble like a guard (he started as one in high school before springing to 6-foot-10) or drop back for a three

and run the court with elegance and power. And of course, there's that 7-foot-5 wingspan. Despite a shoulder injury that kept him out of the lineup for five games in late February, the 21-year-old returned with a bang, registering 39 points, 13 boards and 8 blocks in an 88–85 win versus Detroit. He followed that up in mid-March with another ludicrous line that nearly nabbed him a quadruple double—36 points, 14 rebounds, 7 assists and 9 blocks.

It's a foregone conclusion that Davis will be a perennial All-Star. The question many are asking is how many trophies will this guy win?

CAREER HIGHLIGHTS

- Named an NBA All-Rookie (First Team) in 2012–13
- Has played in two All-Star Games (2014, 2015)
- Won an Olympic gold medal with the U.S. men's basketball team in London in 2012
- Led the league in blocks per game in 2013–14 (2.8) and 2014–15 (2.9)
- Led the NBA in two-point field goals in 2014–15 (641)

TORONTO RAPTORS

POSITION SHOOTING GUARD / **SHOOTS** RIGHT / **HEIGHT** 6'7" / **WEIGHT** 220 LB. / **DRAFTED** 2009, TORONTO RAPTORS, 9TH OVERALL

DEMAR DEROZAN 10

IT'S BEEN HARD to label DeMar DeRozan a superstar quite yet, difficult to mention him in the company of NBA greats. But slowly, surely, quietly and diligently, the face of the Toronto Raptors has been putting in work, and it's finally paying off for the shooting guard, both in career numbers and team success for the Raptors.

Even at 6-foot-7, DeRozan's athletic frame appears more compact and lean than oversized. The product of Compton High School and USC, DeRozan has always surprised pundits with his smooth dribbling, sweet jumper and knack for getting to the line. But make no mistake, he's always been lethal, and as a high school freshman he averaged 26.1 points and 8.4 rebounds. He was so gifted that not only could he dunk at 12 years old, but even the gang members in his neighborhood chose not to mess with the family of the talented young man who stayed loyal to his hometown high school rather than jumping ship for a more prestigious place to play.

Forgoing the final three years of his NCAA eligibility after one season at USC, where he was named Pac-10 tournament MVP, the athletic guard was selected by the Toronto Raptors ninth overall in 2009. While other players have shunned playing in Canada or elected to move elsewhere to pursue better opportunities to win after their entry-level contracts were complete, DeRozan has stepped up. Toronto was where he wanted to be, and despite several losing seasons to begin his tenure, the last few years have paid dividends, and DeRozan's emerged as a leader and the go-to guy on the team.

His size on the defensive end against smaller guards is difficult to get past, and he can guard undersized forwards on the wing, a versatility hard to find in the NBA.

CAREER HIGHLIGHTS

- Drafted by the Toronto Raptors in the first round (9th overall) in 2009
- Played in the 2014 NBA All-Star Game
- Named NBA Player of the Month for April 2015
- Won a gold medal with the U.S. men's basketball team at the 2014 World Cup in Spain
- Set career single-game highs in points (42) and rebounds (11) in 2014–15

against Brooklyn, DeRozan upped the ante, contributing 23.9 per game and shooting 89.9 percent from the free-throw line, while playing 40-plus minutes per night alongside point guard Kyle Lowry, and the two revealed themselves as one of the better backcourts in the game.

Over the past five seasons, DeRozan has been a horse, logging nearly 35 minutes per contest. In 2014–15, however, he faced his first lengthy layoff after tearing an adductor muscle, which forced him out for 21 games. And although it took some time to find his form, DeRozan propped up the Raptors while the team battled injuries and inconsistent play. In March DeRozan dropped a cool 35 on the lowly Philadelphia 76ers and then followed that up with 25 against Cleveland. He has become the guy the Raptors want taking shots late in the game, staring down opponents and going 1-on-1 with the shot clock winding down. A quiet confidence oozes from his eyes, a steely look that means business, the look of a cold-blooded killer ready to do it again. You see it in the eyes of the NBA's best, and the Raptors guard is forcing commentators to include him in that category as his career stretches on.

If there's one knock against the six-year pro, it's his three-point shooting, which has climbed only once over the 30 percent mark. But there's no need to add that to his arsenal yet—he's still slashing and driving, turning around defenders with a crossover and draining difficult turnaround Js. And all that pressure helps him make it to the line. He put an exclamation mark on the 2014–15 regular season when he went toe to toe with MVP runner-up James Harden in late March, posting 42 points and 11 boards in a Raptors home win, both career highs.

If he hasn't come into his own already, DeRozan's about to stand at the peak and look off into the distance because he's finally risen to the top of the mountain. With a second straight playoff berth, a bright future looms in Toronto. And it all hinges on the boy from Compton who decided to call Canada his second home.

From the line, DeRozan is equally dangerous, averaging over 80 percent from the stripe and making teams pay for hacking at his arms as he nimbly darts to the hoop. He put up career numbers in 2013–14, leading the Raptors to the playoffs for the first time in five years. His 22.7 points per game went along with 4.3 boards and 4 assists, and he was top 10 in the league in getting to the line, where he shot 82.4 percent (the third highest completion percentage of the group of 10). In the seven-game playoff series

CLEVELAND CAVALIERS

POSITION POINT GUARD / **SHOOTS** RIGHT / **HEIGHT** 6'3" / **WEIGHT** 193 LB. / **DRAFTED** 2011, CLEVELAND CAVALIERS, 1ST OVERALL

KYRIE IRVING [2]

THE TALENT IS there. The personality is too. What Kyrie Irving needs to become one of the greatest stars in the NBA is to take the always elusive next step. And after the success he had in 2014–15, when the 23-year-old point guard dropped two 50-point games—among other highlights—he may have finally arrived.

Irving's path to stardom isn't run of the mill. He was born in Melbourne, Australia, and raised in New Jersey. His father played professionally down under before relocating to the Garden State, where the younger Irving flourished. Irving owes a lot to his father, who failed to make the NBA but ensured his son would, stating boldly that Kyrie be the best player in New Jersey. The positive thinking wore off: Irving, who was dribbling a ball at just 13 months old, wrote himself a note in fourth grade that said "GOAL: PLAY IN THE NBA."

First he went to Duke, where he played just 11 games his first season because of a toe injury. By then, even with the limited college trial, everyone knew the talented guard. In a classic case of one-and-done, Irving declared for the draft and was selected first overall by the Cleveland Cavaliers. In his rookie season he averaged 18.5 points per game, 5.4 assists and a shooting percentage of .469 en route to Rookie of the Year honors despite missing 15 games. But playing for a hapless Cavs team wasn't ideal for the rising star, and the team finished with a 21-45 record.

His point-per-game totals increased the following season by a whopping 4 points, but the Cavs still failed to make waves in the Eastern Conference. Soon he'd not only be swimming with sharks, he was

the shark. In the 2013–14 All-Star Game, Irving chucked up 31 points and dished out 14 assists on the way to being named MVP. That same season he posted the first triple-double of his career against the Utah

Jazz with a line of 21 points, 12 assists and 10 rebounds. He was beginning to impress the league with his scoring punch and consistency, and he also garnered attention for his famous "Uncle Drew" character in Pepsi Max commercials.

However, Irving's career will probably be remembered in two distinct phases: pre-LeBron and post-LeBron. With the arrival in Cleveland of the four-time MVP to start the 2014–15 season, Irving hit the jackpot. His career averages saw only a slight uptick with James in the mix, but with the explosive forward gobbling up the majority of attention from defenders, Irving is now given time to shine in ways he wasn't before. He is the Cavs' driving force, the straw that stirs the drink. He is a shifty point guard with top-level dribbling skills capable of running the floor, dishing the rock or stepping back to hit a timely trey. Take the night that Irving, with LeBron nursing a wrist injury, stung the talent-heavy Portland Trail Blazers for 55 points in a 99–94 win. Irving sunk 11 three-pointers and went a perfect 10 for 10 from the stripe in what was then a career high for points. Not to be outdone by even himself, the point guard upped the ante and sent a message to the entire league with his 57-point performance against the reigning-champion San Antonio Spurs on nationwide television. "The kid is special," James said following the game. Charles Barkley called it "one of the best individual performances I've ever seen."

But it's not only LeBron who's made Cleveland a better squad since Irving's rookie season—the addition of Kevin Love, Mike Miller and Tristan Thompson makes this a talent-laden, veteran-heavy team and a perennial contender in the East. The 2014–15 season saw the Cavs make it all the way to Game 6 of the NBA Finals, despite a knee injury to Irving in Game 1. Irving averaged 19 points, 3.8 assists and 3.9 rebounds over 13 playoff games and was sorely missed as a three-point threat in the finals (he'd been shooting 45 percent).

It's an exciting time to be Irving. He weathered some lean years in Cleveland to begin his career, and now the team's poised to compete for the near future in a weak Eastern Conference. With a young, healthy Irving and a dominant, still-in-his-prime LeBron, Cleveland fans are hoping this recent NBA Finals appearance is the first of many.

CAREER HIGHLIGHTS

- Named NBA Rookie of the Year for 2011–12
- Named the All-Star Game MVP in 2013–14
- Named an NBA All-Rookie (First Team) in 2011–12
- Named NBA Rookie of the Month three times in 2011–12
- Has played in three All-Star Games (2013–2015)

PORTLAND TRAIL BLAZERS

POSITION POINT GUARD / **SHOOTS** RIGHT / **HEIGHT** 6'3" / **WEIGHT** 195 LB. / **DRAFTED** 2012, PORTLAND TRAIL BLAZERS, 6TH OVERALL

DAMIAN LILLARD ⁰

DAMIAN LILLARD SHOULD need no introduction to anyone who has watched the Portland Trail Blazers play during the past three years. The point guard from Oakland has firmly established himself as the future of the franchise and one of the rising stars in the NBA.

The most impressive thing you can call a basketball player is clutch. And that's what Lillard proved himself to be in the 2014 playoffs, ending a long drought for Portland fans who'd been waiting to see their team travel beyond the first round. Some have called his game-winning basket in Game 6 versus the Houston Rockets the greatest shot in Trail Blazers history. Lillard's heroics cemented the first playoff series win in 14 years and endeared him to a fan base starving for a championship.

Nights like that will define Lillard's career for years to come. He grew up tough and quickly—you have to on the streets of Oakland. With that toughness came an obsession—he was always at the gym as a kid, looking for a game. His older brother once described him as "fearless." But Lillard was undersized and, in his own words in 2012, "overlooked." Few scholarship offers from big schools came his way, and he opted to attend Weber State in Utah, a mid-major that's not exactly on the national radar. But with a tenacity and scoring ability that saw him post 24.5 points, 5 rebounds and 4 assists per game, he was propelled to the top of the ranks by his

junior season, and he skipped senior year to head into the draft, where the Trail Blazers grabbed him with the sixth pick in 2012. It was a steal.

Slow to make a name for himself out of high school, he wasted no time as a professional, entering the NBA with a bang. Lillard put up 23 points and 11 assists in his debut and never looked back, torching the league in his rookie campaign. He finished with 19 points, 6.5 assists and 3.1 rebounds per game and was a unanimous decision for Rookie of the Year. Playing all 82 games for the second straight season in his sophomore campaign (2013–14), Lillard proved his inaugural season was no fluke, posting nearly identical numbers and increasing his threat to score from behind the arc to nearly 40 percent. He made the All-Star Team and dropped 41 points against the Sacramento Kings. And then came the playoff run, where he scored 22.9 points per contest, assisting at a rate of 6.5 per game and adding 5.1 rebounds. And of course there was that inimitable shot that sent "Rip City" into a frenzy.

With just 0.9 seconds on the clock and down 98–96 to the Houston Rockets, the Trail Blazers drew up a play for Nic Batum to inbound the ball to center LaMarcus Aldridge and go for the tie. Lillard, being guarded by Chandler Parsons at the right wing, looked almost disinterested as he played possum behind the screens of his fellow players awaiting the inbounds pass. His first step fooled Parsons, and he headed toward the top of the key, wide open, clapping for the ball. Batum said after the game about the change of plans: "He was too open. I had to."

Lillard got the ball, set his feet and gracefully and quickly released a perfect arc of a shot before Parsons could contest it. Nothing but net. Pandemonium ensued, and Lillard rightfully peacocked around the crowded court, thumping his chest all the way into Trail Blazers history after hitting the shot of his life.

The 2014–15 season was nearly identical for Lillard. The 6-foot-3 point guard averaged nearly 36 minutes per night and routinely put up 20-plus points. In early December, Lillard hit 7 of 11 from three-point land against the Chicago Bulls en route to a 35-point outing. Two games later versus the San Antonio Spurs, he hauled

down 10 boards to go along with 23 points, 6 assists, 2 steals and a perfect 6 of 6 from the stripe. When the teams met again a week later, his 43 points led all scorers in a triple OT thriller. And those clutch stats? Through his first 14 career OT games, he went 29 of 41 field goals attempted (70.7 percent), 10 of 18 three-point field goals attempted (55.6 percent) and 15 of 16 free throws attempted (93.8 percent).

Lillard, if you haven't realized, is a big-time budding star. If he can keep delivering, he's going to keep sending fans in Rip City into a frenzy year after year.

CAREER HIGHLIGHTS

- Named NBA Rookie of the Year for 2012–13
- Named an NBA All-Rookie (First Team) in 2012–13
- Has played in two All-Star Games (2014, 2015)
- Led the NBA in minutes played in 2012–13 (3167)
- Led the Trail Blazers in points in all three seasons with them (2012–13 to 2014–15)

CLEVELAND CAVALIERS

POSITION POWER FORWARD–CENTER / **SHOOTS** RIGHT / **HEIGHT** 6'10" / **WEIGHT** 243 LB. / **DRAFTED** 2008, MEMPHIS GRIZZLIES, 5TH OVERALL

KEVIN LOVE 0

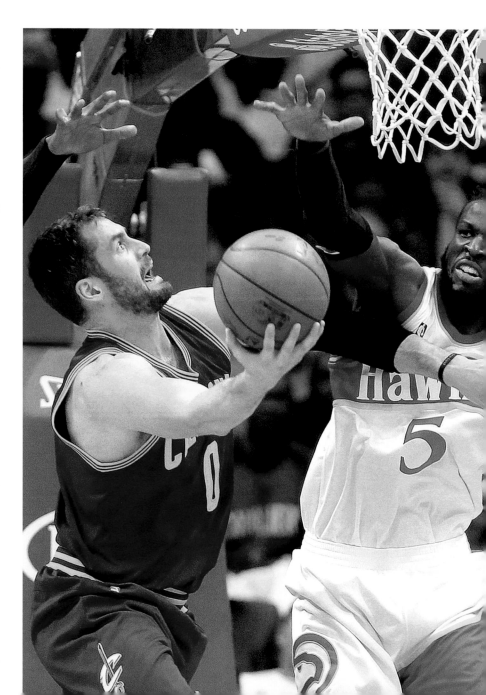

A PRODUCT OF Lake Oswego High School in Oregon, Kevin Love was destined for the NBA. The prodigy took the west coast state by storm upon arriving in high school as a 6-foot-8 monster of a teenager. As a sophomore, he was a man among boys and once scored 50 points and 20 rebounds in one game. He led Lake Oswego to a state championship in his junior season, and during his final year, he averaged 33.9 points per game and 17 boards. That's what you call dominant.

Love's only year at UCLA was equally so. He accrued 17.5 points per game, 10.6 rebounds and a .565 field goal percentage while taking the Bruins to the 2008 Final Four alongside Russell Westbrook. The Bruins lost to the Derrick Rose–led Memphis Tigers. It would be Love's only year at college, as he declared for the draft and was taken by the Memphis Grizzlies fifth overall. Subsequently traded to the Minnesota Timberwolves, he established himself quickly, becoming one of the scariest power forwards in the game under coach Rick Adelman.

At 6-foot-10 and 243 pounds, Love's inside strength is obvious and his rebounding prowess legendary. But it's also his deft touch from 20 feet out that makes him a threat from all points on the court. And when he gets to the line, he's made over 80 percent of his free throws thus far in his career. On November 12, 2010, history was made, and Love was the centerpiece. The power forward hauled down 31 boards to go with 31 points against the New York Knicks. It was the first 30-30 game in the NBA in 28 years—since Moses Malone hit the mark in 1982. It was the most rebounds in a game since a guy named Charles Barkley accomplished the feat, and Love's teammate at the time, Michael Beasley, even claimed the big forward whispered to him Babe Ruth–like on the bench, "I'm going for 30 tonight." Later that season he posted a line of 43 points and 17 boards, then smoothly followed that up with a 37-23 game. He led the NBA in rebounding in 2010–11 with 15.2 boards per game.

Despite Love's stellar play, the Timberwolves were a team in decline, and following 2013–14, when he put up arguably his best season to date—26.1 points, 12.5 boards and 4.4 assists (a career best) while shooting a respectable 45.7 percent from the field—Love made it known he wanted out.

Superstar LeBron James just happened to be making his own move, and Love became a focal point as the four-time MVP returned to Cleveland. James had played with Love in the 2012 Olympics and convinced his international teammate to forgo an offer to be a building block on a rebuilding Los Angeles Lakers squad and instead help him bring a championship to Cleveland.

With two number one picks in Andrew Wiggins and Anthony Bennett coming back to the Wolves in a three-team deal that also included Philadelphia, Love landed in Ohio with James, and the two of them joined crafty, bucket-slashing point guard Kyrie Irving to form the East's most explosive troika.

So far in Cleveland, though, it's been a learning curve for Love—sharing the rock doesn't come easily to the big man who likes to have the ball flow through him. Logically, playing with LeBron means Love's numbers are down—and in some cases, such as points per game, way down. But he's in Ohio for one thing and one thing only—to win a ring. He still put up 22 points and 19 boards versus Charlotte in December and routinely started going

20-10 after that. He finished the season with 38 double-doubles, tied for 10th most in 2014–15 and best on the Cavaliers.

A shoulder injury in the first round of the playoffs at the hands of Boston Celtics center Kelly Olynyk derailed Love's season, and he played no part in the Cavs' finals run. With a fresh five-year, $110-million deal to hang with LeBron and company in Cleveland, the 26-year-old ball hawk has plenty of prime years left to establish a legacy as a winner in Ohio. For Cavs fans, it would be money well spent.

CAREER HIGHLIGHTS

- Named NBA Most Improved Player for 2010–11
- Named an NBA All-Rookie (Second Team) in 2008–09
- Has played in three All-Star Games (2011, 2012, 2014)
- Has been in the top 10 of total rebounds since his rookie season, including leading the league in 2010–11
- Is second on the list of active NBA players for rebounds per game (11.8)

ATLANTA HAWKS

POSITION POINT GUARD / **SHOOTS** RIGHT / **HEIGHT** 6'2" / **WEIGHT** 180 LB. / **DRAFTED** 2009, ATLANTA HAWKS, 19TH OVERALL

JEFF TEAGUE⁰

IF YOU HAVEN'T been paying attention, Jeff Teague has quietly been taking the South by storm, leading the Atlanta Hawks to first place in the Eastern Conference in the 2014–15 season. Along the way, Teague has become one of the most consistent players in the NBA thanks to his blend of speed, passing ability and unselfish leadership

Teague was selected by the Hawks 19th overall in the 2009 draft after two standout seasons at Wake Forest, the alma mater of another legendary point guard, Chris Paul. And Teague comes from point guard pedigree—his father, Shawn "Happy" Teague, was a standout college player in the early 1980s with a Rick Pitino–led Boston University. Happy's career flamed out—his son's is burning up.

Completing his sixth season with the Hawks, Teague's finally rounded into form, and in each of the past four seasons he's improved his point totals. His career started slowly—just 10 starts in his first two seasons, watching idly as teammate Josh Smith, a hometowner who played nine seasons in Atlanta, hucked up shots in what some referred to as an isolation offense. "I didn't cut. I didn't slash. I didn't move with the ball," Teague said of his early years with the team.

The point guard's talents were going to waste in Atlanta. By season three, his points per game had increased to 12.6 to go with 4.9 assists, thanks to his starting status, but the system wasn't suited to his

CAREER HIGHLIGHTS

- Played in the 2015 NBA All-Star Game
- Led the Atlanta Hawks to the 2015 Eastern Conference final (19.3 points, 5.0 assists)
- Shot 95 percent from the free-throw line in the 2015 playoffs
- Set a career high in points (34) in 2013–14
- Is a two-time NBA Player of the Week

game. In 2012–13, he upped his assist total to 7.2 per game and shot 88.1 percent from the charity stripe while recording a career-high 15 double-doubles, but the Hawks were still running their offense through Smith. The following season, a changing of the guard occurred, as the Hawks let Smith go to Detroit in free agency. It was finally Teague's team, and with a new coach installed the same year, it's never been the same in Atlanta. This season alone the Hawks produced four All-Stars.

"What's unique about [Teague]," said coach Mike Budenholzer, "is his ability to pass." And once he handed the keys to his new primary point guard, Teague was off, cutting and slashing to his heart's content. And that suited Budenholzer, a former assistant in San Antonio, just fine. His model for Teague is Spurs superstar Tony Parker: the cutting, slashing, play-off-a-million-screens European point guard who is a whirling dervish on the hardcourt.

At 26 years of age, Teague's just coming

into his own. With the Hawks cresting to the top of the NBA peak with their magical 60-22 season (one that included a 19-game winning streak), Teague looks poised to be captaining a perennial favorite alongside sterling lieutenants Al Horford and Paul Millsap. All three averaged more than 15 points per contest in 2014–15, showcasing how well the Hawks share the ball. (All five Atlanta starters averaged more than 12 points.) In an NBA where a single franchise star typically rules the roost, the Hawks are an anomaly and Teague is the quiet leader, averaging 15.9 points, 7 assists and 2.5 boards over the regular season. Highlights included an early five-game streak of 23 points or more, as well as a 25 point, 8 assist, 7 rebound performance against Milwaukee in the first game after Christmas. During the winning streak in January, he hit double figures in assists five times. He shot nearly 90 percent from the free-throw line in February. He also finished top 10 in the league in helpers.

Best of all, the Hawks made it all the way to the Eastern Conference finals—the first time the franchise made it that deep since the 1970–71 season.

Since he's become a starter, Teague has figured out how to find his bigs on the pick and roll and high screens instead of settling for long-range jumpers, something he was guilty of during his early tenure. Now the player wearing number zero has joined the ranks of do-it-all backcourt generals around the NBA—guys who incorporate a double threat of scoring and passing to ensure success. If 2014–15 is any indication, NBA fans have witnessed the birth of a star.

POSITION POINT GUARD / **SHOOTS** RIGHT / **HEIGHT** 6'4" / **WEIGHT** 195 LB. / **DRAFTED** 2010, WASHINGTON WIZARDS, 1ST OVERALL

JOHN WALL 2

SOME PLAYERS JUST can't seem to get a fair shake—they are good, even great, but perhaps not superstar great. That could be a product of playing in a certain era, or simply the fault of high expectations. Either way, John Wall's firmly been in the category of not getting enough respect. And that's about to change.

Wall's as pure a point guard as they come: lightning-quick first step, excellent shot, deadly passer. The latter was especially true in the 2014–15 season when he averaged 10 assists per game—second behind Chris Paul—en route to a starting All-Star appearance (his second). With Wall's recent leadership, the Washington Wizards are firmly a playoff contender. Teammates like Bradley Beal and Marcin Gortat don't hurt either, but it's Wall's magic that stokes the engine of the team, and he's finally getting his due.

The 6-foot-4 guard didn't have a typical childhood—his father was incarcerated just after John was born and passed away when he was just nine. Wall was a tempestuous kid on and off the court in his hometown of Raleigh, North Carolina, and the kids took to calling him "Crazy J." Anger issues made several coaches ban him from high-level basketball camps when he was a teenager. But he finally got his act together, and by the time he graduated, he led his team to the state championship, averaging 19.7 points, 9 assists and just over 8 rebounds. His speed is undeniable, Iverson-esque, and his high school coach claims he clocked him at 3.5 seconds from end line to end line when Wall was still a teenager.

He was a one-and-done at the University of Kentucky, putting up 16.6 points and 6.5 dimes per contest before he was selected first overall by the Wizards in the 2010 draft. He recorded a triple-double six

- Named an NBA All-Rookie (First Team) in 2010–11
- Named to NBA All-Defensive Second Team in 2014–15
- Has played in two All-Star Games (2014, 2015)
- Led the NBA in assists in 2013–14 (721)
- Ranks second in assists per game among active NBA players (8.7)

he did. It might be hard to imagine such a once-selfish person on the basketball court becoming one of the league's most unselfish players. But that is exactly what Wall did— and how he led the Wizards out of the NBA hinterlands.

He's averaging nearly 9 assists per game during his career and has emerged as a basketball player masquerading as an artist: he drives down the lane and spins 360 for layups; throws behind-the-back passes to teammates; startles opponents with a "yo-yo" dribble and a fake pass that creates space for him and his teammates.

He began the 2014–15 season with two 30-point affairs in the first five games. In November he posted 5 steals against Milwaukee. He recorded 17 assists twice in December and started that month with seven straight games of 10-plus assists, putting up only one game of fewer than 8 helpers. Or how about that 19-point, 16-assist game versus Denver in January? Or his 28 points, 12 assists and 8 rebounds later that month against Toronto? By the All-Star break, he was leading the team in points, assists and steals, the same as he did in 2013–14. It's hard to imagine where the Wizards would be without the former Kentucky product hoisting this team on his back, especially in the first round of the playoffs, when he torched the Toronto Raptors during a four-game sweep, with 26 points and 17 assists in Game 2 and 19 and 15 the following game. He was quite simply an unstoppable force, whether racing down the court on a fast break, finding Marcin Gortat in the paint or dishing to Bradley Beal on the wing for a trey. But a wrist fracture at the beginning of the second round forced him to the bench, and despite a valiant return later in the series, the Wizards were bounced by the Atlanta Hawks.

Long gone is the ghost of Gilbert Arenas, a one-time superstar in Washington with a massive contract who fizzled out. In his stead is the man with quick hands and faster feet, who has quietly become one of the best guards in the game today and who just might be the first to bring a championship to Washington in over 35 years.

games into his rookie season (19 points, 13 assists and 10 rebounds), but the Wizards were simply horrible, losing 59 games. They lost 46 in the lockout-shortened 2011–12 season and 59 again the following year. Some players may have gotten used to all the losing. Not Wall. Not a kid who came from the rough Raleigh projects like

CLUTCH
PERFORMANCES

BASKETBALL IS REALLY quite simple. It's a quick, high-scoring game, with relentless up-and-down, back-and-forth action on the court. Twelve to a team. Five on the floor. Ten total. It's a sport played in two 24-minute halves and four 12-minute quarters. At times it's as complex as a high-screen pick and roll followed by a kick-out to the weak side for an open three, and sometimes it's simply one man versus another, mano a mano, with the clock winding down and nothing standing in the way but Father Time, a chance at immortality waiting.

Since James Naismith nailed two opposing peach baskets to the walls of a gymnasium in Springfield, Massachusetts, in 1891, the question of clutch has arisen in boardrooms, back rooms and barrooms. Clutch is a measuring stick in the NBA by which men are judged and careers defined. In basketball, being clutch is everything.

There are clutch performers in every sport—the gunslinger QB in football, the shutdown goalie in hockey and the walk-off hitter in baseball. In basketball, clutch means a whole host of different things, but it is best encapsulated in one moment, one shot, one game, with everything on the line. Who emerges from the fray? Who, among the 10 men on the court, distinguishes himself in a league full of giants in a game that may be the last of the season? An athlete faces no greater test, no greater purpose, than rising to

The Portland Trail Blazers' Damian Lillard, center, is mobbed by teammates after nailing a series-winning buzzer beater against the Houston Rockets in 2014.

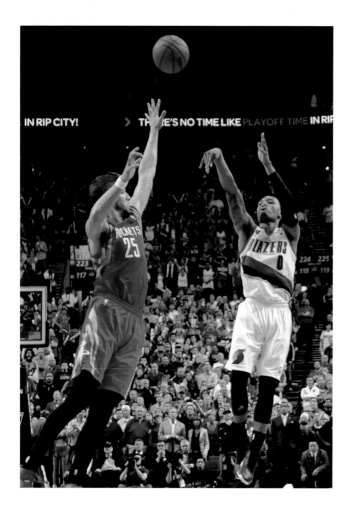

IN RIP CITY! ▶ THERE'S NO TIME LIKE PLAYOFF TIME IN RIP

Portland's Damian Lillard watches his series-winning shot against the Houston Rockets' Chandler Parsons in 2014. The shot sent the Trail Blazers into the second round of the playoffs for the first time in 14 years.

But clutch moments also come in entire-game performances, not just instants in the waning moments of a game. Take Magic Johnson's Game 6 performance in the 1980s finals, where the rookie point guard started at center in lieu of Kareem Abdul-Jabbar and casually contributed 42 points, 15 boards and 7 assists while going 14 for 14 from the line in 47 minutes. In 2012, ESPN ranked Magic's night number two all-time for single-game performances. And don't forget the legendary Bill Russell's ridiculous 10-0 record in Game 7s, capped off by a 30-point, 40-rebound performance in 1962. Michael Jordan was so clutch he didn't even need a Game 7 in any of the finals he played in. He claimed MVP of the NBA Finals six times—that's called rising to the occasion on the biggest stage possible, over and over again.

With the advance of analytics, the definition of clutch is being rewritten, and the new math is contributing in a macro sense to a better understanding of a player's worth on the court. Perhaps, though, it's reducing the way we approach the micro—there's still something magical about that game-winning shot or jaw-dropping jam, even if it's seen via six-second Vine on our smartphones. There's still something powerful about watching greatness explode off the dribble, perfection rising off the floor and magic floating toward the basket in slow motion. The thrill of witnessing "clutch" manifest is bigger than victory itself. It doesn't matter if you don't remember the details. You'll remember how it made you feel: one man, one bucket, nothing but net.

THE SHOT

Poor Craig Ehlo. His Cleveland Cavaliers were a rising power in the Eastern Conference and had drawn the Chicago Bulls in the first round of the 1989 playoffs. It was Jordan's fifth NBA season, and the Bulls had never advanced past the first round since he'd arrived. Cleveland had finished 6-0 versus the Bulls that year in the regular season, finishing third to Chicago's sixth place. Cleveland was the clear favorite and Jordan and the Bulls the underdog.

In the final game of the best-of-five first round, with three seconds left on the clock, Jordan pushed through the screen, grabbed the inbounds pass and made toward the top of the key, a half step ahead of Ehlo. People forget Jordan wasn't a game-ending legend until that bucket in Game 5. From 15 feet he rose up to shoot. Ehlo jumped and reached up and flew by as Jordan hovered a moment longer than Ehlo could hang with him, and Jordan hit the rising shot over Ehlo's disappearing fingers as the clock hit zero and the Bulls clinched the series. The lasting image of Jordan jumping into the air, pumping his fist and beating his chest, is as famous as the shot that inspired the celebration.

Ehlo became so defined by Jordan's moment that when the former Cavs forward recently entered a rehab facility for addiction to painkillers following back surgery, a kid recognized him as the guy who was guarding Jordan. Some nights, some plays, some games, good or bad, define you. They follow you everywhere. They become part of the larger basketball narrative. Ehlo's last words before the

the challenge in the final minutes or seconds of a deciding game.

Clutch also happens to be susceptible to the way we choose to remember things. With so many seasons, so many players and so many incredible moments, it's hard to recall what happened when. What year? What team? What shot? And even though memory-making moments now emerge more readily thanks to instant replay and 24/7 sports channels, the moments etched in NBA lore are the ones we choose to remember best. It could be the player, the circumstance or the feat itself—but like most things in life, not all clutch moments are created equal.

Take Jordan's push-off, fadeaway dagger over Byron Russell to seal the 1998 finals, or Larry Bird's steal with seconds left in the 1987 Eastern Conference final against Isiah Thomas and the Detroit Pistons that won the Celtics the game. Every market has a franchise-defining moment. For the championship-starved Portland Trail Blazers, Damian Lillard's series clincher on home court in the first round of the 2013–14 playoffs versus the Houston Rockets wasn't just a series winner. It was history for the fans in Portland.

Reggie Miller taunts New York Knicks celebrity fan Spike Lee after scoring 8 points in the final 18.7 seconds to steal Game 1 of the 1995 Eastern Conference semifinal.

inbounds—"Mr. Jordan, I can't let you score"—add drama to the story. Poor Craig Ehlo.

It says something when one of the most clutch moments in NBA history involves two players. When a basketball play becomes known as "the Shot," something has captured the imagination of basketball fans. Jordan's make, even though it didn't lead to a title that year, became the emotional hump the Bulls franchise needed to become NBA champions in 1991. Maybe that is why the Shot etched its way into the global consciousness.

As far as buzzer-beating, series-ending shots go, it's hard not to put the Shot up there as one of the greatest of all time. The Bulls would go on to beat the Cavs five times over a seven-year span in the play-offs. LeBron James and company exacted some revenge this past season by slaying the Chicago dragon that has so often breathed fire on the Cleveland basketball community.

REGGIE AT MSG

Sometimes it's not a playoff winning shot, though. It's more than that. It's a deep rivalry that pits one man against an entire city. That man is Reggie Miller, and the city? Where else but New York.

On May 7, 1995, nine seconds felt like a lifetime for Knicks fans. It was the Indiana Pacers Reggie again. Reggie at Madison Square Garden again. The same Reggie who put up 25 in the fourth quarter of Game 5 in the 1994 conference finals the year prior, a ridiculous performance that drew the ire of fans from across all five boroughs. The same Reggie who returned to MSG to exact revenge for losing that series and missing a chance to compete in the 1994 NBA Finals. And it would be the same Reggie who, in Game 1 of the 1995 Eastern Conference finals, put a dagger through the hearts of New Yorkers that night in May, in just nine seconds, cementing his ruthless, road-killer persona for years to come.

Few NBA players ignited a firestorm in a road building like Miller. Film director Spike Lee sat courtside and provided the perfect people's champ—a passionate celebrity fan with New York street cred who lived and died with the Knicks.

The back-and-forth trash talk between spectator and player was a legendary sideshow to the Indiana–New York rivalry, providing a perfect backdrop for "Miller Time." The Knicks, up by six with 18.7 seconds to go in Game 1, held a seemingly impossible lead. But Miller came down the floor and coolly knocked down a three to cut the lead in half. The guard then improbably stole the ball off the inbounds, and in a moment of complete cold-blooded hubris, he backpedaled behind the arc instead of going for the easy layup that would have cut the lead to one. He drained it, tying the game. The Knicks' John Starks then missed two free throws at the other end, and Miller came back down the court, was fouled and ended up at the line himself. In the span of nine seconds, the Knicks had gone from six points up to down by two, all in their home building at the hands of one man. Reggie.

As the buzzer sounded, Miller began mugging at Lee, grabbing

Larry Bird celebrates Boston's one-point victory over the Detroit Pistons in the fifth game of the 1987 Eastern Conference finals. Bird stole the inbounds pass that sealed the win for Boston.

his own neck. He yelled, "Choke artists!" while running into the tunnel following the robbery of Game 1, and the episode became immortalized in the 30 for 30 documentary entitled *Winner Time*. Time and time again, Miller saved his best for MSG—countless playoff performances that stunned the crowd and cemented a lifelong beef with Lee. Six playoff series over a span of seven years will do that. But it was those eight points in nine seconds in Game 1 of the 1995 Eastern Conference finals that everyone remembers as one of the deadliest clutch performances in NBA history.

LARRY BIRD

But sometimes clutch isn't just one game. It's a career's worth of highlights that define a player's clutch worthiness. One such man is "the Hick from French Lick," Larry Bird.

Legendary not only for his shot but also for his trash talk, Bird was unassailable. He once told Xavier McDaniel exactly where he would be on the court after a time-out before hitting the game-winner. One evening, he hit a game-winning shot with Jordan, no slouch on D, right in his face.

Upon winning his third three-point shootout in a row at the NBA All-Star Game, Bird's iconic finger was raised in the air as soon as the ball left his hands—he knew he'd won in a moment reminiscent of Babe Ruth's called shot. And of course there was the steal, probably the most famous steal of all time, when Bird snatched Isiah Thomas' inbounds pass, fed the ball to Dennis Johnson and won Game 5 of the 1987 Eastern Conference finals with his defense. He didn't just want to beat you—he wanted to destroy you, squeeze you into submission, ensure you cried on your way home because you couldn't contend with greatness.

Bird may not have as many game-winners on the highlight reel as other players, but he was iconically clutch, winning three NBA championships in the 1980s—twice named the finals MVP, three times in a row the regular-season MVP. There was a stretch in the 80s when he was simply unstoppable. In 1984–85, Bird did it all: 28.7 points a game, 10.5 rebounds, 6.6 assists and .427 from three-point land. He was an 88 percent free-throw shooter, not

even his career high. In his third-last year at 34 years old, he shot 93 percent from the stripe, 21st all-time for one season, and he currently stands 11th all-time behind Reggie Miller. He didn't leave the league as a leader in any major categories, but his reputation was greater than that. Jordan, when asked once who he'd pick to take the final shot, didn't hesitate: Larry Bird.

STEPH CURRY

If there's one player in the NBA currently holding the mantle for most clutch player in the league, it's not even close: Steph Curry. Yes, he's young. Yes, there are other more established superstars like Kobe and LeBron. But Kobe is on the brink of retirement, LeBron's catalog of buzzer beaters is thin, and a crop of young, big-time stars such as Curry is emerging around the league.

In his short tenure so far, Curry's past few seasons have proven he's the purest shooter in the NBA, the biggest threat from behind the arc and perhaps the least clutch-looking guy on the court with

Stephen Curry, who scored 26 of his game-high 40 points after the start of the third quarter, celebrates Golden State's 123–119 overtime victory over the New Orleans Pelicans in Game 3 of their 2015 first-round series.

that mouth guard wagging from his lips. He's not tall—6-foot-3 on a good day—and he's slight. Not skinny necessarily, just slight-looking, a far cry from the trash-talking of Jordan and the mean-mugging of Bryant. He's a favorite of the analytics crowd, too. Curry plays admirable defense for an offensive threat and a smaller guard, ranking high in SportVU and real plus–minus, and he finished fourth in steals in 2014–15. He also shot 686 three-pointers, making 286, ranking him fourth with just over a .440 shooting percentage despite hucking up 100 more shots than the next man, teammate Klay Thompson. He demolished Miller's playoff record of 58 threes by launching 98 over the course of the Warriors' championship run.

He's also deadly in the final seconds of a game. In Game 3 of the first round of the 2014–15 playoffs versus the New Orleans Pelicans, the Warriors, up two games but down 20 on the road in the fourth quarter, mounted an unimaginable comeback, conducted by none other than their maestro, Curry, whose fallaway three with seconds left sent the game into overtime. It was on the Internet before he could peel his body off the court. Curry hit the final two free throws for 40 points total to secure the win. (He finished with 39 the next game as they swept the Pelicans.) It was symbolic of

everything clutch—despite a cold start, he caught fire at the end of a playoff game, knocking down bucket after bucket until the ultimate shot. He would be named regular-season MVP days later.

Carmelo, Kobe, LeBron, even Durant—keep 'em—Curry is the guy down one, down three, down 20 who gets the ball.

THE AGE OF ANALYTICS

The definition of clutch shooting is going through a transitional phase as analytics become a source of information to fans and GMs in an attempt to gather the true value of a player to his team. Video cameras are ubiquitous devices in NBA arenas these days— SportVU cameras in the rafters, specifically, track every player's movement for the entire game. Sure, coaches still scratch Xs and Os on the sidelines during a time-out. But the real work is being done in dark rooms, far beyond the reaches of the court, where data gets sent from those cameras, which were installed at the beginning of the 2013–14 season. Statisticians and newly hired data analysts then review mountains of data. It's complicated stuff—most stats guys are professors or PhD students in economics and do not come from a sports background. But they're massive basketball pioneers on the frontier of applying science to the hardcourt.

Shooting charts are growing in popularity and are easily available online. Phrases like "expected performance value," or EPV, are creeping into the casual fan's vocabulary, and stats like PER (player efficiency rating) and true shooting percentage are already mainstream

on sites like basketball-reference.com. Adjusted plus–minus, or real plus–minus, is another stat gaining momentum on ESPN. Dallas Mavericks owner Mark Cuban told ESPN earlier this year that "Analytics have been an important part of who we are since I walked in the door 15 years ago. We have strived to introduce new and exclusive sources of data so that we can improve performance of our players." Those PhD guys are even introducing papers that attempt to explain defensive worth on the basketball court, tracking and analyzing "counterpoints," which, according to Grantland, "estimate how many points an individual defender allows per 100 possessions."

Alexander Franks and Andrew Miller, the authors of the study,

Houston Rockets center Dwight Howard, left, and guard James Harden are the darlings of the analytics movement and a dream combo for the Rockets.

suggest Chris Paul is the top defensive point guard in the league after crunching the numbers. Although it seems obvious to the naked eye that Paul is pretty money without the ball, the numbers now back it up, and we are entering territory that the assistant vice president of Stats LLC called "the ability to measure the impact individual defenders are having throughout the game," a huge leap forward for the NBA. Paul's reputation as a winner has taken a hit over his career, thanks to few playoff series wins until this season. That changed when Paul willed the Clippers past the reigning-champion

Chris Paul steals the ball from LA's Nick Young in 2014–15. Paul led the NBA in steals that season; it was his sixth time leading the league in the stat.

San Antonio Spurs in a thrilling Game 7 victory in the first round of the 2015 playoffs, and his game-ending shot, off-balance with Tim Duncan's hand in his face, should silence his critics. The point is: it's easy to see Paul's worth when he nets a series winner. Those SportVU cameras will record not only where Paul was on the court, and the two points that counted on the scoreboard, but also how he fared throughout the game. Beyond well-known players like Paul, general managers will use advanced statistics to identify undervalued players who add an element to the game beyond baskets.

Several GMs now come from an analytics background, including Houston Rockets head honcho Daryl Morey and Sam Hinkie, the Philadelphia 76ers guru who is turning heads with his unconventional moves. The Rockets were the first team in the NBA to hire a cadre of stats guys in the front office to give them an edge. On the court, the team is led by James Harden and Dwight Howard, and the Rockets have all but eliminated a midrange jump shot from their offensive attack, taking an inordinate number of threes or shots in the paint not only because the stats back it up but also because the assembled personnel provide a reason to. If Harden or any of his backcourt counterparts miss one of their umpteen threes, guess who's there to gobble up the board? Howard, only one of the best rebounders in the game.

Not everyone, however, has embraced the new era of statistical data. This season Charles Barkley called Morey "one of those idiots who believes in analytics." The Lakers, Knicks and Nets have been well behind the eight ball in embracing the philosophy of numbers, and the Knicks and Lakers—unsurprisingly based on the advanced statistics—finished in the top five of field goal attempts made from 15 to 19 feet. In other words, they took a lot of poor probability midrange shots. The Rockets? They were dead last in this category.

So what does it say about the way we're understanding clutch? Maybe we're moving past the highlight-reel buzzer beater into the realm where a player's complete skill set comes into play over a longer period of time. Quantifying stats may not be the sexiest way to understand a basketball player's worth, but it's growing in popularity. At the very least, for stats geeks around the world, it's provided an arsenal for debate at the bar when Harden pulls up for another three, or Andrea Bargnani settles for a long-range jumper instead of attacking the rim.

The way we understand the game has certainly changed, and players like Harden and Russell Westbrook are being coveted in the draft. As a point guard coming out of college, Westbrook had his size and assist rate challenged. But Seattle/Oklahoma's brass saw an opportunity, and after his MVP-like season in 2014–15, where he carried the Thunder in every category while Kevin Durant was on the sideline, the Thunder brass, and their analytics team, are looking like geniuses in identifying superstar talent.

There will always be obvious choices every draft. Andrew Wiggins and Jabari Parker were automatic top two selections in the 2014 draft. Jahlil Okafor of Duke, the number three pick in the 2015 draft, is a lock to be a solid NBA player. The trick is using analytics to go further. It's those teams at five through 10 who should be using everything available to make value judgments on future NBA players.

WE'VE COME A long way since Mr. Naismith, in that old gymnasium in 1891, recalled a game from his Canadian childhood named "Duck on a Rock" and went about creating the rules for a new game he'd call "Basket Ball." From no backboards and a closed hoop, we've arrived at a time and place that includes dozens of in-arena cameras, SportVU and the uber-analysis of the game at a second-by-second level. It's impossible to think what Naismith would have thought about all this technology. It doesn't mean that anything has irrevocably changed since Naismith wrote his first 13 rules—the game is fundamentally the same. There are still 10 men on the court, five a side, with the goal to put the ball in the opponent's basket. And what will never go away is that last-minute shot, the anticipation as the clock ticks down that one man is getting the ball and one man is defending him. One of them will walk off the court, head shaking. The other, arms raised, a hero.

ANDREW WIGGINS

LOS ANGELES LAKERS

POSITION POINT GUARD / **SHOOTS** RIGHT / **HEIGHT** 6'5" / **WEIGHT** 185 LB. / **DRAFTED** 2014, WASHINGTON WIZARDS, 46TH OVERALL

JORDAN CLARKSON 6

IN A LOADED rookie class, Jordan Clarkson certainly felt under the radar to begin the season, especially in the mentee role behind superstar Kobe Bryant. But another injury to the fading Hall of Famer opened a door for the first-year guard, and he thrived in 2014–15 for the rebuilding Los Angeles Lakers.

Born to an American military father and Filipino mother, Clarkson is part of a new wave of players in the NBA that are adding to the growing mosaic of multiculturalism around the league. Raised in San Antonio, Texas, he played several seasons for the University of Tulsa before transferring to Missouri, where he showcased his skill set to NBA scouts, dropping 17.5 points per game in his final year of college ball. He even scalded powerhouse Kentucky for 28 points and appeared well on his way to a first-round selection in the 2014 NBA Draft. But after his father's cancer diagnosis, Clarkson's play dropped off, as did his hopes for an early draft spot. His father recovered, and Clarkson was selected 46th overall by the Washington Wizards, who quickly traded him to the Lakers thanks to already owning a powerhouse backcourt in John Wall and Bradley Beal. The trade is now looking like an outright steal for the storied California franchise. The Lakers were looking to add a guard to complement seventh overall pick and power forward Julius Randle, who sat out the previous year with a knee injury suffered early in the season.

At 6-foot-5 and 185 pounds, Clarkson has a great blend of size and speed and can shift between both guard spots if needed. For now, he'll likely remain in the point guard position, with Bryant still playing shooting guard. Clarkson possesses a strong rim attack, and his ball-handling skills—praised by everyone around him—are perfect for dishing on the slash or heading to the line for a few freebies. Carlos Boozer referred to Clarkson as "Baby Westbrook." He's also a highly motivated player, and after a poor outing, he rewatched the NBA Draft multiple times to serve as inspiration for his next game. That act is either really badass or extremely masochistic.

If one good thing came out of the debacle that was Steve Nash's injury-riddled two seasons in LA, it's that the former two-time MVP was around to influence the Lakers' young core, including Clarkson, specifically offering him tips on creating space.

Clarkson started 38 games out of 59 during his rookie season, many of those during the second half with Bryant out. And he took full advantage of the opportunity, finishing February by averaging nearly 14 points, 4 dimes and a steal per contest, while shooting 85 percent from the line. Late in the season, he scored a career-high 30 points and added 7 assists to punctuate his coming-out party, following it up four games later with a fierce 26 points, 11 helpers and 6 boards against the Sixers, one of only two wins out of the last 10 for the Lakers as they finished out a horrendous season.

And although he finished seventh in Rookie of the Year voting, he's become one to watch as the 27-55 Lakers retool the franchise and go young. Among rookies, Clarkson finished second in points per game with 11.9 behind Rookie of the Year Wiggins, third in assists and top 10 in free throw and field goal percentage. Those totals are all excellent signs that among a strong crop of first-year players, he's capable of playing at a high level night in and night out if given the opportunity.

But that will be the question moving forward. Everyone knows Kobe needs the ball, and the Lakers may feel the need to improve at the point guard position by adding a veteran. One writer called Clarkson "the lone bright spot" on an otherwise dismal team. Lakers GM Mitch Kupchak wants Clarkson to bulk up, no surprise considering his slight frame and

the daunting 82-game NBA season. He also wants Clarkson to practice playing off the ball, alluding to the notion that the young guard may shift between the one and the two positions.

Although he may not have been a high draft pick, Clarkson is proving his detractors wrong and remains an inexpensive option at point guard for the near future. His price, his attitude and, above all, his revelatory play have shown he may be a piece of the puzzle in Hollywood for a long, long time.

CAREER HIGHLIGHTS

- Named an NBA All-Rookie (First Team) in 2014–15
- Named Rookie of the Month in March 2015
- Finished second in rookie scoring (11.9) in 2014–15
- Finished third in rookie assists (3.5) in 2014–15
- Finished fourth in rookie free-throw percentage (.829) in 2014–15

POSITION SHOOTING GUARD / **SHOOTS** RIGHT / **HEIGHT** 6'6" / **WEIGHT** 190 LB. / **DRAFTED** 2014, UTAH JAZZ, 5TH OVERALL

DANTE EXUM¹¹

LIKE MOST ROOKIES in the NBA, Dante Exum is a work in progress. Still, Exum's a little different from the others. The Australian's an outlier to many North Americans, and after playing his first season in Utah, the 6-foot-6 guard may still be an unknown. What is known? He possesses an oil well's worth of talent, and the Utah Jazz are going to be cautious in their approach to the next big thing.

The fifth overall selection in the 2014 draft, the 19-year-old entered the league ready to play if not excel. With his length and ability to shift between both guard spots, the potential to be great is there; after a full season with the Jazz, that potential is really what Utah fans will drool over.

Exum was born to hardcourt pedigree—his father Cecil played college ball alongside two of the greats, Michael Jordan and James Worthy, and all three won the 1982 NCAA Championship with the North Carolina Tar Heels. But his father shipped off to the land down under, fashioning an admirable career and raising his son to be NBA-ready.

The good news: Exum played in all 82 games in 2014–15, starting 41. The not-so-good news: his numbers didn't explode like those of surefire number one pick Andrew Wiggins, and he finished the year with averages of 4.8 points, 2.4 assists and 1.6 rebounds per game in 22 minutes of action, good for 10th among rookies. In March, he expressed the frustration of a first-year player who was a standout in high school. "I've always been a guy that's had the ball in his hands most of the time, at the end of the shot clock, end of the game." But he understands his place on the Jazz and is humble enough to accept the "backseat role." Another thing he acknowledges is the need to be more aggressive—he took only 32 free throws all season, and the sheer size of NBA players in the paint may have been a deterrent. And although the guard's offensive numbers didn't flash, his awareness on the back end was a revelation, proving he possesses both a high basketball IQ and the tenacity needed to be effective on the floor against quicker guards.

He notched 15 points in January against the Milwaukee Bucks in 35 minutes, hitting 5 of 10 from behind the arc, which appears to be where he's going to make his living for the near future, though to be a consistent threat, he'll need to improve on his 31 percent three-point shooting percentage. During a six-game winning streak in March, he hit double digits in points three times, proving each time he can be an effective threat from three-point range. What he's missing is a slash move to the rim and a willingness to bang bodies in the paint. Despite his lack of a drive game, Exum can still dish the rock. In one late performance during the season, he put up 12 assists, a career high, in a tidy 29 minutes versus the Denver Nuggets, and he finished eighth among rookie assist leaders.

It's going to take time, but the Jazz have a solid nucleus moving forward with small forward Gordon Hayward up front and shot-blocker Rudy Gobert on defense. The Jazz are young—no player on last year's roster was older than 27. So adding a veteran presence is a must for the rebuilding franchise. They finished only 38-44, which in the mighty Western Conference isn't good enough, but in the East could have earned them a playoff berth—the Brooklyn Nets finished eighth with an identical record. At one point late in the season, the Jazz rifled off 13 wins in 16 contests, so there's hope in Salt Lake.

Exum possesses the talent and the work ethic to excel in the NBA. It's a matter of putting it all together. In a strong rookie class, the kid from down under might have a slow climb to the top.

CAREER HIGHLIGHTS

- Drafted by the Utah Jazz in the first round (5th overall) in 2014
- Set a career high in points (15) in January 2015
- Set a career high in assists (12) in April 2015
- Finished eighth in rookie assists (2.4) for 2014–15
- Was named to the 2013 FIBA U19 All-Tournament Team

POSITION SHOOTING GUARD–POINT GUARD / **SHOOTS** RIGHT / **HEIGHT** 6'5" / **WEIGHT** 183 LB. / **DRAFTED** 2014, MINNESOTA TIMBERWOLVES, 13TH OVERALL

ZACH LAVINE 8

ZACH LAVINE IS dirty. As in dirty good. He may have gone unnoticed when the 2014–15 season began in his role as the Minnesota Timberwolves freshman not named Wiggins, but ever since his high-flying antics at the 2015 NBA All-Star Game, LaVine has proven he's one to watch.

At 6-foot-5 and 183 pounds, the shooting guard doesn't cut an imposing figure, but his talent level is off the charts. The Wolves needed athleticism—they'd yet to swing the deal with Cleveland for number one pick Andrew Wiggins—and coveted the UCLA product. What they got by selecting LaVine 13th overall was a multiposition guard who at just 20 years old is proving he possesses a higher ceiling than people may have thought.

LaVine grew up in the Northwest, the son of a former football player. One of Washington State's best high school players, he jumped to the college scene, suiting up for the UCLA Bruins. He lasted only a year and wasn't even one of the best players on the team. But, boy, the kid could dunk (he sports a rumored one-step 46-inch vertical).

"Thank God for the Internet" must have been what every basketball fan muttered when LaVine showed up at the 2015 Slam Dunk Contest. Inside the Barclay's Center in Brooklyn, in the biggest city in North America, LaVine could not have picked a better or bigger arena to showcase his bag of tricks. Wearing the "Toon Squad" No. 23 jersey from the movie Space Jam—an hom-

age to Michael Jordan—LaVine entered the arena to the theme song from the movie. It was nothing if not hubristic, but the kid from Washington walked the walk,

demolishing the competition. Victor Oladipo, his closest competitor, never stood a chance. Mason Plumlee looked like a pylon next to LaVine's high-flying antics.

His first dunk: between the legs. His second: behind the back. Both spectacular. All four of his dunks were executed at a high degree of difficulty, but most importantly LaVine had the crowd and a crew of NBA superstars on the sidelines jumping out of their seats. It was the most exciting dunk contest since Vince Carter brought the house down in 2000, and it has helped elevate LaVine's status around the league. He is the opposite of the quiet Wiggins, an outgoing, confident personality his coach Flip Saunders calls a "city mouse." Wiggins, by contrast, is the team's "country mouse."

LaVine's 2014–15 season, stats-wise, is certainly something to sniff at. Finishing with 10.1 points, 3.6 assists and 2.8 rebounds, he was a solid contributor who was rewarded with increased playing time as the year went on. When point guard Ricky Rubio was lost to injury, LaVine gobbled up the minutes, playing out of his usual position but not looking out of position. One thing's certain: LaVine has stamina—in back-to-back OT games at the end of March, he played 46 and 48 minutes, respectively. He averaged 40 minutes per night over the final eight games, and 25 minutes per game throughout the year.

LaVine had many highlights outside the Slam Dunk Contest in his rookie campaign. In November, he poured in 28 versus Kobe Bryant and the LA Lakers. Days later he dished 10 dimes against San Antonio to go along with 22 points. Versus the Golden State Warriors, another of the NBA's elite and home to the Splash Brothers, Steph Curry and Klay Thompson, he racked up a career-high 14 assists. In April—again against the Warriors and with just days to go in the season—LaVine saved his best for last, going off for 37 points, knocking down 6 of 10 threes on 13-of-21 shooting from the field, and adding 9 boards and 4 helpers. He finished second in rookie free-throw percentage, fifth in rookie scoring and eighth in rookie shooting percentage from behind the arc.

Saunders was impressed, stating at the end of the season, "Anytime . . . you can go through a stretch where you can play 10 games, [and] you can average 20 a game, that's impressive."

Admittedly cocky, the league's top dunker still has a little work to do to become prime time. But if he can put on weight so he can muscle through screens, and if he commits to working on his defense, LaVine will be a great number two with Wiggins.

The one-two punch could even set up to be the NBA's next Splash Brothers.

CAREER HIGHLIGHTS

- Drafted by the Minnesota Timberwolves in the first round (13th overall) in 2014
- Named an NBA All-Rookie (Second Team) in 2014–15
- Won the NBA Slam Dunk Contest in 2015
- Finished second in rookie assists (3.6) in 2014–15
- Finished fifth in rookie scoring (10.1) in 2014–15

HOUSTON ROCKETS

POSITION SHOOTING GUARD / **SHOOTS** RIGHT / **HEIGHT** 6'6" / **WEIGHT** 205 LB. / **DRAFTED** 2014, PHILADELPHIA 76ERS, 32ND OVERALL

K.J. MCDANIELS 32

K.J. MCDANIELS IS arriving. It may not be tomorrow, or the next day, but he's coming. Now in the Houston Rockets organization after a trade deadline deal sent him packing his bags from Philadelphia, where he was selected 32nd in the 2014 draft, McDaniels will be out to prove he can become an integral piece of the puzzle on a franchise with title aspirations.

In three years at Clemson, the 6-foot-6 shooting guard did it all. First and foremost, he was one of the most feared shot-blockers in the ACC, registering 2.8 per game in his junior year. (It's a trait he's carried to the NBA, where as a midsized guard logging just over 20 minutes per game, he's been able to average a little more than 1 block.)

At Clemson he also contributed 17.1 points per game and 7.1 rebounds and was named ACC Defensive Player of the Year in 2014. At one point, he was the only player in Division I to lead his team in five very different categories: scoring, rebounding, steals, blocks and threes. And thanks to a supportive extended family that traveled to see him play in college, McDaniels thrived at Clemson. But they also pushed him; and older, bigger cousins who lived in Mobile, Alabama, didn't let up on the prospect. It also helped that his father played college ball, making the NCAA tournament in 1991 with the University of South Alabama.

According to his mother's scouting report McDaniels is a "beast" on the court,

"but off the court, he's so kind and gentle and humble." That may explain his love for dogs, especially pit bull terriers, with whom he has a special affinity.

McDaniels started his NBA career on fire: in his 52 games with the 76ers, he averaged 9.2 points per contest. Some of his early highlights include 21 points and 13 rebounds against the Dallas Mavericks and a 10-point, 8-rebound and 4-block affair versus the Toronto Raptors. He compiled seven games with 3 blocks or more—his most memorable stuff coming against the Raptors early in the season. With the Sixers down 23 points in the third quarter, McDaniels absolutely spiked the ball into the premium seats on a Greivis Vasquez floater, accidentally concussing a woman in the stands (he later sent her flowers). It was just his seventh NBA game. He torched the NBA during November from behind the arc, going 39.5 percent, and over the course of the year shot 75 percent from the line. By the end of the season his points per game total dipped to 7.9, but it was still good for a top-10 rookie finish.

McDaniels, who felt he should have been a first-round pick, gambled with the Sixers—instead of signing a long-term rookie deal, the shooting guard opted for a one-year contract, figuring his raw athleticism would be coveted once he had a chance to showcase himself in the NBA.

Getting plucked by the Rockets has its benefits: the number-savvy franchise will certainly appreciate McDaniels' versatility and will work with him on the ways he can make the most impact on the floor. But it also comes with drawbacks, namely, less playing time. The Rockets have a deep squad, and for McDaniels that meant going from 27 minutes a game in January to riding the pine—in the final two months of the season he only played 33 minutes total. It could be argued that the Rockets underused him and could have benefitted from his defense in the playoffs, especially against the high-flying LA Clippers, who pushed Houston to seven games before the Rockets ultimately won.

McDaniels has near-limitless potential,

and NBA teams are always in line for defensive-minded players. But where he fits on Houston is a question mark for the talented rookie from Birmingham, Alabama. At shooting guard, he'll never get the minutes backing up MVP candidate James Harden, so he'll likely shift to the three and play small forward, where, with his leaping ability, he won't be too undersized. He's got all the tools, but whether he can put together the kit is another question. One thing is certain: whether above the rim or below, McDaniels will be soaring.

CAREER HIGHLIGHTS

- Drafted by the Philadelphia 76ers in the second round (32nd overall) in 2014
- Recorded a double-double of 23 points and 13 rebounds in November 2014
- Averaged 1.1 blocks per game in 2014–15
- Finished second in rookie blocks (1.13) and 10th in rookie scoring (7.9) in 2014–15
- Was ACC Defensive Player of the Year for 2013–14

NERLENS NOEL [4]

THERE WEREN'T A lot of bright spots in the 2014–15 season for the Philadelphia 76ers. They came out of the gate with a 17-game losing streak and appeared headed for one of the worst seasons in NBA history. But one man emerged as the future for this lackluster squad, easily identifiable with his hi-top fade haircut. Rookie star Nerlens Noel, at 6-foot-11 and 228 pounds, is poised to lead this franchise out of the darkness and into the Promised Land, one basket at a time.

The son of hardworking Haitian immigrants, Noel was a massive prospect in the Boston area at Everett High before he even set foot on a college court. In 2012, his high school senior year, he was named top player in the USA, and he finished his senior season on scholarship with the prestigious Tilton School in New Hampshire after being heavily recruited away from his hometown. Before he'd even reached the NBA, the *New York Times* hailed him as "the best shot-blocker of his generation."

Playing nearly the entire 2014–15 NBA season, and starting most games, it's been a trial by fire for the 22-year-old from Massachusetts. He suited up just one year for the storied Kentucky program before he was drafted sixth overall by the New Orleans Pelicans in 2013. Following the draft, he was traded to the Sixers for Jrue Holiday. But he missed a year after tearing his ACL and didn't dress until 2014–15. His numbers at Kentucky were impressive though—10.5 points, 9.5 rebounds and an unreal 4.4 blocks.

He finished his rookie season averaging 9.9 points and 8.1 rebounds to go along with a solid 1.9 blocks per game, eighth in the league. It was an impressive showing for a freshman, especially one who missed an entire season of basketball. In addition, his 1.8 steals is incredible for a big man, and he finished with more than 100 blocks and 100 steals, a rare feat achieved in the NBA. His massive 7-foot-4 wingspan, quickness and leaping ability are causing havoc for opposing teams, and the league is finally seeing the attributes Noel carried with him throughout high school and college. Comparisons to Patrick Ewing, David Robinson and Hakeem Olajuwon have followed him, and it's showing.

In just the second game of his rookie year, Noel put up 14 points and 10 boards. A month later, he posted 17 and 12 versus the New York Knicks in 39 minutes on the floor. By March, Noels had rounded into form, averaging 14.3 points per game during the month and 11.2 rebounds. In February, he was a beast, recording 12 points, 9 boards and 9 blocks against the Indiana Pacers, just missing the elusive blocks-inclusive

CAREER HIGHLIGHTS

- Named an NBA All-Rookie (First Team) in 2014–15
- Recorded 9 blocks versus the Indiana Pacers in February 2015
- Finished eighth in the NBA in blocks per game (1.9) and total blocks (142) in 2014–15
- Led all rookies in rebounding (8.1) in 2014–15
- Finished sixth in rookie scoring (9.9) in 2014–15

triple-double. In his most productive offensive game that season against the Los Angeles Clippers, he went for 30 points and 14 off the glass on 12-of-17 shooting, big numbers for a rookie center. Most impressive? On March 20, he became the youngest player in NBA history to record 20 points, 10 rebounds, 5 steals and 3 blocks in a game. His coach, after a game in late March, called Noels a "game-changer" after the center put up a cool 14 points, 10 rebounds and 6 stuffs.

And although he wasn't Rookie of the Year—he finished third—he certainly turned heads, particularly late in the season, making voters take notice that it wasn't a one-horse race with Andrew Wiggins in

pole position. He led all first-year players in rebounds, blocks and steals, and if he improves his offensive skill set even a little bit in the off-season, he may be poised to become a truly unique talent, more like a Joakim Noah than Ewing.

The Sixers lost their last 10 games in 2014–15, and coupled with that early 17-game losing streak, that's going to be tough on a talent like Noels. But his attitude and haircut—which has its own Twitter account—are trending positive. If the sly Sixers brass can cobble together a few extra pieces in the coming years to complement their high-flying defensive backbone, we may be looking back at this season as the beginning of something truly special.

JABARI PARKER 12

RAISED ON THE south side of Chicago, Jabari Parker was born a basketball stud, ballooning to nearly 6 feet tall by fifth grade largely thanks to the genetics he inherited from his basketball-playing father, who spent six seasons in the NBA in the 1970s, averaging 10 points per game.

In high school, the Mormon-raised Parker won four Illinois state championships with the Simeon Career Academy, a prep school famous for producing another NBA star, Derrick Rose. Parker was so touted that he started as a freshman (something Rose never did). He did the little things at age 14 that make players great later in life, like carrying the water for the sophomore team, or requesting the coach be harder on him in front of the other players so Parker's teammates didn't think the prodigy was getting special treatment. By senior year, McDonald's and Gatorade named him their High School Player of the Year.

Parker landed at Duke to play for Coach K, and his numbers in his only year there were spectacular—19.1 points, 8.7 rebounds, 1.2 assists, 1.2 steals and 35 percent from behind the line. His moves in the post and consistent jump shot were hailed as head and shoulders above his competition, and it was a foregone conclusion that Parker was NBA-ready. The only question that remained was just where he would go in the draft.

In one of the strongest draft classes in recent years, Parker was selected second

his personality off the court. His Mormon background—unusual for an African-American from Chicago—has made him a humble, well-liked teammate. A former Duke professor called Parker "very wise for one so young. A philosopher's soul in an athlete's body."

Despite his 6-foot-8, 240-pound frame, his rookie season wasn't without its proverbial bumps and bruises, not to mention literal ones as the teenager came up against grown men in the paint. Several times in the first 10 games his coach, former NBA player Jason Kidd, benched his star pupil. Although Parker wasn't a model of consistency, he showed flashes of brilliance. He dropped 18 points, 5 rebounds and 3 steals against the Detroit Pistons in just 28 minutes in early November, and he posted several double-doubles in the inaugural month of the season, including two in his first three games. But a devastating knee injury in December sidelined him for the remainder of the season. Owing to a positive attitude following the diagnosis of an ACL tear, Parker resolved to "stay optimistic" and looked forward to a "brand-new knee." He finished his rookie season with just 25 games under his belt, but his per-game numbers were impressive nonetheless—12.3 points, 5.3 boards, 1.7 assists and 1.24 steals—and he was named Eastern Conference Rookie of the Month for October and November.

No one doubts his toolkit is there. Former Bulls coach Tom Thibodeau said at the start of the 2014–15 season: "He's a load. A tough matchup. He can shoot, put it on the floor, play in the post, pass. Move without the ball. Those guys are hard to guard. He's going to be a great pro."

Parker's destined to be a star, and for years to come he should anchor a young Milwaukee squad that is loaded with talent, including Giannis Antetokounmpo and newly acquired Michael Carter-Williams. With Milwaukee a short drive from Chicago, it's a perfect fit for the family-oriented Parker. In time, he may be the most well-rounded big man in the league since Tim Duncan.

overall by the Milwaukee Bucks in 2014 behind Canadian phenom Andrew Wiggins. Both started for their respective clubs, and Parker now has a chance to prove he should have been number one. The Bucks don't mind though—they've acquired a long, strong power forward who should stabilize the franchise up front for years to come. The Bucks may have salivated not only at his athletic prowess but also at

POSITION POINT GUARD / **SHOOTS** RIGHT / **HEIGHT** 6'4" / **WEIGHT** 185 LB. / **DRAFTED** 2014, PHILADELPHIA 76ERS, 10TH OVERALL

ELFRID PAYTON ⁴

ELFRID PAYTON, WITH his signature curls and flashy play, established himself as one of the NBA's top freshmen in 2014–15. The Orlando Magic rookie is the son of a former Canadian Football League player with the same name. Payton Sr. was a tireless Hall of Fame defensive end who amassed 154 sacks over his career. His son possesses a similar gift: a passion to compete. The Paytons lived in Gretna, just outside of New Orleans, and they were forced to leave the city after Hurricane Katrina. Elfrid was in seventh grade and played football, but shortly after the move he abandoned his father's chosen sport for basketball. It was a good decision, as he's fast becoming a top point guard in the NBA.

Payton's strong play in his rookie season garnered him praise, but it didn't turn the tide in Orlando, where the Magic, a young, enthusiastic squad, went 25-57. There is reason for optimism, though, especially with a young core that includes stud center Nik Vucevic, high-flying dunker Vladimir Oladipo and 2014 lottery pick Aaron Gordon, who missed half the season because of injury. Helming the ship is Payton, the 6-foot-4 point guard with a 6-foot-8 wingspan, who was the 10th pick in the 2014 draft.

It's looking like a steal. Payton—with rangy arms, impressive ball handling and a willingness to attack any defender—has proved difficult to deal with. Prior to the draft, several agents remarked to one GM they didn't want their players working out

with Payton because "he disrupts everything." His college coach, Bob Marlin, said: "He's a super penetrator who plays with both a chip on his shoulder and extreme confidence. Elfrid's got his Dad's fire as well as a maturity."

The point guard played three years for a small school, Louisiana-Lafayette, leading the Ragin' Cajuns into the 2014 NCAA tournament and landing Payton on the national radar. He'd already played with the

CAREER HIGHLIGHTS

- Drafted by the Philadelphia 76ers in the first round (10th overall) in 2014
- Named an NBA All-Rookie (First Team) in 2014–15
- Finished first in rookie assists (6.5) in 2014–15
- Finished second in rookie steals (1.73) in 2014–15
- Finished eighth in rookie rebounding (4.3) and in rookie scoring (8.9) in 2014–15

big boys at the 2013 FIBA U-19 tournament alongside current Celtics rookie Marcus Smart and 2015 lottery pick Jahlil Okafor, winning gold for the USA. But 2014 was Payton's coming-out party.

The Ragin' Cajuns knocked off Georgia State in the Sun Belt Final to arrive as the 14th seed in the NCAA tourney, losing to Doug McDermott and the Creighton Bluejays (McDermott, selected one pick behind Payton, dropped 30 points in the contest). Payton, for his part, notched 24 points, 8 rebounds and 3 assists. In his final regular season of college, he had solid per-game numbers—19.2 points, 6 rebounds, 5.9 assists and 2.3 steals. And college pundits started referring to him before the draft as

a "sleeper." Payton, not short on confidence, called himself "the best point guard in the draft. Just a leader."

So far he's been absolutely right. The rookie played in all 82 games during the 2014–15 season, starting 63 and averaging 30 minutes a night, the fourth most for a first-year player, heeding his father's early advice of "Don't let anyone outwork you." He finished top 10 in rookie scoring with 8.9 points per game. He finished first by a country mile in rookie assists with an average of 6.5, showcasing his dish-first skills to a strong, young frontcourt anchored by an emerging star in Nik Vucevic. He was second in rookie steals (13th league-wide) and should continue to pose a huge threat on the defensive end as one of the best in the league at his position. Payton also had twelve double-doubles, highlighted by triple-doubles in back-to-back games in March versus the Dallas Mavericks and Portland Trail Blazers—no other rookie had a single triple-double. By the end of the season, the Magic were vastly improved and a tough win for opponents. But a stretch in early 2015 garnered only three

wins in 21 games, including a 10-game losing streak, and the coach was fired.

In 13 games, Payton registered 10 assists or more. He's not the NBA's best long-range shooter by any stretch, but that's not his game. He strangles opponents on D, pushes the pace up the court, possesses a slick crossover and has strong rebounding for a point guard. Above all, he brings tough leadership—an intangible that often breeds a winning culture.

The whole package led to a third-place finish in Rookie of the Year voting.

Orlando is a long way away from the days of Anfernee Hardaway and Shaquille O'Neal, but for the first time in a long time, the future is bright and sunny for the Magic. It starts with Payton, the fulcrum of the offense, the backbone of the defense and above all a leader on a young team that's making strides to contend again. There's something enigmatic about the 21-year-old point guard, a cool confidence that radiates outward to his teammates. If his first year's any indication, Payton should be leading the Magic into the playoffs before the rabbit's even out of the hat.

POSITION POINT GUARD / SHOOTS RIGHT / HEIGHT 6'4" / WEIGHT 220 LB. / DRAFTED 2014, BOSTON CELTICS, 6TH OVERALL

MARCUS SMART 36

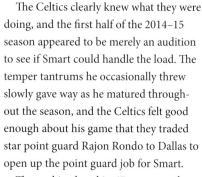

THERE ARE A few reasons why the Boston Celtics, in a rebuilding year, made the NBA playoffs this past season. The main one? The emergence of rookie Marcus Smart, who is fast becoming one of the great young guards in the game today. Possessing an array of skills under and above the rim, the future looks bright for Smart in Beantown.

It wasn't the easiest of childhoods for Smart, growing up in a tough part of Dallas and watching one brother succumb to cancer and two others squander their shots at promising basketball careers. As the youngest Smart brother, Marcus worked hard to make sure he earned his chances, gaining a reputation as a guy willing to take on anything and anyone. He guarded near seven-footers in high school, dunked on boys eight inches taller than him and baited opponents into taking charge after charge. One friend said this of Smart in high school: "I never saw him go half-speed on anything. Even during drills that weren't meaningful." He won two high school state championships, his teams going 115-6 over three seasons.

In his first year at Oklahoma State, Smart was named Big 12 Player of the Year. He could have declared right then and there, but he stayed an additional

season. In his final year he put up 18.9 points, 5.9 rebounds and 4.8 assists, adding 2.9 steals for good measure, making him as complete a guard as they come. The Celtics liked his well-rounded game and took him sixth overall in 2014. For some it may have represented a slight fall not to be selected in the top three, but he was lost in the hoopla behind guaranteed franchise-changers Andrew Wiggins and Jabari Parker. It may have been a good thing.

The Celtics clearly knew what they were doing, and the first half of the 2014–15 season appeared to be merely an audition to see if Smart could handle the load. The temper tantrums he occasionally threw slowly gave way as he matured through-out the season, and the Celtics felt good enough about his game that they traded star point guard Rajon Rondo to Dallas to open up the point guard job for Smart.

The rookie played in 67 games total, starting 38, and clocked in with per-game averages of 7.8 points, 3.3 assists and 3.1 rebounds. But those numbers don't illustrate the big games he had against top teams. In March, Smart drained 25 points against the Oklahoma City Thunder, adding 9 boards and 5 dimes in 37 minutes of work. Then he dropped 19 on 7-of-10 shooting against Cleveland during the last week of the season. Taking over the starting point guard spot on February 3, Smart was a force, especially defensively because of his size at point guard—6-foot-4, 220 pounds—his able footwork and down-right tenacity, and his tough defense. March was the month he really shone, averaging 9.8 points, 4.5 assists and

4.3 rebounds as the Celtics marched toward the playoffs.

His bulldozer-type game is a departure from the finesse game Rondo played, but that works because Smart's counterpart on the Celtics, Isaiah Thomas, provides that element. But Smart's bulldog mentality can get him in trouble, and he's trying to tone it down. Against Oklahoma State, he was suspended several games for getting into a physical altercation with a fan. With the Celtics this year, he sat for one game after hitting San Antonio forward Matt Bonner in the crown jewels.

At only 21, he's the second-youngest player on the current Celtics, and the 2014–15 playoff experience will go a long way in helping shape his game. Smart averaged 9.8 points in four games versus the Cavaliers before the Celtics bowed out, second among rookies in the first round. Under the tutelage of coach Brad Stevens, and with umpteen top picks in the 2015 draft, Boston's positioned for a deep playoff run in a few seasons.

Smart finished top 10 in rookie minutes, 11th in scoring, fifth in assists and third in steals for first-year players. He's kind of a hybrid—a small shooting guard or a huge point guard—and his coach deemed him "physically, mentally and emotionally ahead of the curve" just days before the playoffs began. High praise for a rookie third on the depth chart to start the year. If things continue, the Celtics are going to look like the smart ones.

- Drafted by the Boston Celtics in the first round (6th overall) in 2014
- Named an NBA All-Rookie (Second Team) in 2014–15
- Finished third in rookie steals (1.48) in 2014–15
- Finished fifth in rookie assists (3.1) in 2014–15
- Finished 11th in rookie scoring (7.8) in 2014–15

MINNESOTA TIMBERWOLVES

POSITION SHOOTING GUARD / **SHOOTS** RIGHT / **HEIGHT** 6'8" / **WEIGHT** 199 LB. / **DRAFTED** 2014, CLEVELAND CAVALIERS, 1ST OVERALL

ANDREW WIGGINS 22

NOT MANY NBA rookies have had to deal with as much fame as Canadian Andrew Wiggins. The first overall pick of the 2014 draft has handled the circus with aplomb and grace, qualities sure to be fundamental as he embarks on a long career in the NBA.

Hailing from Toronto, Ontario, the new hotbed of international basketball thanks in part to the success of Vince Carter a decade ago, Wiggins was a rising star as a teenager and was quickly noticed by pundits down south. Like other Canadians before him, he jumped ship for the opportunity to play for the prestigious Huntington Prep High School in West Virginia, an incubator for future NBA talent.

Following his senior year at Huntington, Wiggins shipped off to the University of Kansas for a classic one-and-done experience: promising NBA first-rounders choose schools that will hone their skills for just one year before declaring eligibility. It paid off. All freshman year, Wiggins, under the tutelage of coach Bill Self, was the talk of the NCAA. In 35 games with the Jayhawks, Wiggins averaged a team-high 17.1 points per game, as well as 5.9 rebounds and 1.5 assists. Although the numbers weren't eye-popping across the nation, the fact Wiggins was just 18 years old fueled speculations he'd go first or second overall. Possessing raw athleticism, smooth jumping ability, sound defensive awareness and an otherworldly vertical of 44 inches (among the highest ever recorded), Wiggins was too skilled to let drop to second, and he was drafted by the Cleveland Cavaliers first overall. It appeared Wiggins would play student under the mentorship of LeBron James—a Cavalier again after his triumphant announcement that he was leaving the shores of Miami for his hometown, where he began his career. But the celebration for Wiggins would be short-lived.

Rumors abounded the Cavs were looking

for another piece to their push for a championship—the Minnesota Timberwolves' Kevin Love. Wiggins, however, had signed with the Cavs and could not be traded for a 30-day period owing to a clause in the collective bargaining agreement. Thus, the 19-year-old remained in limbo, a sitting duck until the deal could be formalized. In late August of 2014, Wiggins became only the second number one draft choice since 1976 to never play for the team that drafted him when Cleveland sent Wiggins and fellow Canadian Anthony Bennett to Minnesota for Kevin Love and Thaddeus Young (from Philadelphia), who acquired Alexey Shved, Luc Mbah and Cleveland's number one pick in the 2015 draft.

When the T-Wolves finally introduced Wiggins to the public, he was all smiles. "It's been a crazy summer," he said in August 2014. "But I wanted to play for a team that wanted me." The two Canucks form a formidable one-two north-of-the-border punch for the Minnesota fan base, which should suit them both fine, since Minneapolis is the chilliest city in the NBA (not Toronto, despite the very popular "We The North" campaign). As Wiggins told his former Jayhawks coach Bill Self at the time, "It's better for me . . . to go somewhere where I'm forced to be something."

It might take a year or two for Wiggins to be a bona fide superstar. His first game for Minnesota was largely forgettable (6 points in 19 minutes of play), but he improved throughout the year, recording his first double-double in early December (23 points and 10 assists) in an upset win over the Portland Trail Blazers. On his 20th birthday in late February, he scored 30 points and added 6 boards, proving he possesses the panache to be dominant in the league.

With his first season in the books, Wiggins became the first Timberwolves player to win Rookie of the Year, finishing with 16.9 points and 4.6 rebounds per game. In the final 13 games, he upped his scoring average to 23.3 per contest and started making regular trips to the free-throw line, a good sign he was willing to get dirty for his buckets. Despite a losing season in Minnesota—the team had the worst record in the league—Wiggins proved he can be a go-to option from the perimeter and a basket-attacking force on one end, as well as a defensive stalwart on the other thanks to his enormous wingspan.

Get used to seeing Wiggins and the T-Wolves becoming a dominant presence. With first-overall pick Karl-Anthony Towns joining the squad, Minnesota will be a team to watch.

CAREER HIGHLIGHTS

- Named NBA Rookie of the Year for 2014–15
- Named an NBA All-Rookie (First Team) in 2014–15
- Named Rookie of the Month four times in 2014–15
- Is only the second Canadian to be selected first overall in the NBA draft
- Was the only Timberwolves player in 2014–15 to play all 82 games and score more than 1,300 points; the closest teammate was Zach LaVine with 77 games and 778 points

THE PLAYOFFS

THE REGULAR SEASON is like a warm-up jacket, or a practice jersey, an opening act if you will. Most of the work is done in the lengthy grind, and it does separate the real athletes from the pretenders, but postseason performances are where careers are forged and reputations made. Regardless of regular-season numbers or record-setting seasons, it's rings that matter, not points per game. Whether that's fair or not is another conversation entirely. But in basketball, what separates the good from the great is your ability to come through when it truly matters.

Like the clutch performance conversation, the debate never ceases to double-back on the same questions. Who was the greatest of all time when it mattered most? Who stepped up at a crucial moment? Immortality and everlasting fame, in the annals of sport, art and war, have always been more interesting than one brief moment of glory. Since the days of gladiator pits, the Trojan War and the sacking of cities, having one's name written down in the record books is what lifts men from mere mortals to Gods. Modern times are no different, and in the sport of basketball, the playoffs are king. So what better way to start than with the reigning monarch of the court?

The Miami Heat's LeBron James gestures to the crowd after his team defeated the San Antonio Spurs in 2013 to claim Miami's second straight title.

KING JAMES VERSUS MICHAEL JORDAN

LeBron James—LeBron—the single-name, one-man highlight reel, has succeeded so thoroughly that fans don't even notice how easy he makes it look. A lightning rod for praise and criticism, James has now appeared in five straight finals from 2011 to 2015, the first to do so since Bill Russell made 10 straight from 1957 to 1966. He's won the regular-season MVP award four times, so we know how good a player he is on the march to glory. But what about the finish? With two wins and four losses in six trips, he's been, well, middle of the road with respect to those rings. And of course, it wasn't without controversy that he and Chris Bosh flipped the tables on free agency and agreed to sign with the Miami Heat to join friend and All-Star Dwyane Wade. Manufactured? Sure. But that doesn't dismiss the fact that LeBron led the Heat through four straight seasons and four straight postseasons. That's a lot of wear and tear and playing consistently at a high level, so no wonder he was banged up early in 2014. But as he hits 30 years of age, the discussion has focused less on his choices and more on his legacy, specifically related to Michael Jordan.

LeBron will always be compared with Jordan, no matter how well or poorly he does. A recent ESPN poll said 34 percent of people think Jordan, at 52 years of age, could beat a 30-year-old James, right now, in a game of 1-on-1. That's how wonky and clickbait-driven the debate can get. Perhaps one-third of the public might need to be reminded that LeBron continues to bust up Jordan's numbers.

In the third round of the 2014–15 playoffs against the Atlanta Hawks, James eclipsed Jordan's record of 51 games with at least 30 points, 5 rebounds and 5 assists. Kobe, the next closest, has a mere 37 to his name, and he's played in 220 playoff games compared to LeBron's 178. In Game 3 of that series, with both Kevin Love and Kyrie Irving injured, James scored 38 points, pulled 18 off the glass and dished out 13 assists for the triple-double, all the while hobbled by injuries to his ankle and back and suffering from cramping. And he started the game 0 for 10 from the field! No player has ever posted a line like that, regular season or postseason. The closest? Charles Barkley back in 1993, who stuck 43 points, 15 boards and 10 dimes in Game 5 of the Western Conference finals.

Michael Jordan cradles the NBA championship trophy in 1993 following the Chicago Bulls' 99–98 win over the Phoenix Suns for their third straight title.

LeBron recently passed Kareem Abdul-Jabbar and Jerry West for 30-plus-point playoff games (now third all-time) and sits second behind Magic Johnson for most triple-doubles in the postseason, who it should be mentioned, feels more comparable than Jordan ever will be.

Despite all this, LeBron's had to somehow work harder to outlive the legacy of Jordan. It's likely very simple: MJ never lost in the finals, going 6-0. LeBron, just by losing in the NBA Finals, draws the ire of purists. In 2015, James almost equaled Jordan's 1993 record for highest percentage of his team's points, 38.4 percent to 38.3. However, he long ago shattered Jordan's best PER of 32.04 with a mark of 37.39 (2009), which is second all-time to Jordan's draft mate, Hakeem Olajuwon (38.96).

When James launched himself up from the corner in the dying seconds of Game 4 of the 2015 Conference semifinals versus the Chicago Bulls, it was the third playoff buzzer beater of his career, which many were quick to point out is in fact the same number Michael Jordan has, and yet His Airness' buzzer beaters are somehow legend. James' first: Game 2 of the 2008–09 Eastern Conference finals against the Orlando Magic. With one second on the clock he drained a shot from three-point land to secure victory. James and the Cavaliers eventually lost that series, but LeBron did just about everything over the course of six games: 38.5 points, 8.3 rebounds, 8.3 assists, 49 percent from the field, all in 44.3 minutes a game. That is some next-level business, but the performance is largely forgotten, as is his PER from that entire playoffs.

Conversely, what isn't soon to fade from memory is Jordan's series-ender versus Cleveland in 1989, a touchstone moment in his career. His finals-finisher a decade later in 1998 was just as great, when in Game 6, he sealed the deal on the Bulls' sixth and last ring with a 20-foot jumper with five seconds left. It wasn't technically a buzzer beater, but considering the circumstances, it was just as big. Plus, what's likely forgotten about that 1998 final is that in the 87–86 Game 6 win, Jordan scored a crucial bucket with a minute to go and then stole the ball from Karl Malone to set up the final points. It would be his last title, and probably the lasting image of a great career despite several comebacks and several retirements.

For James, many may remember the 2014–15 NBA Finals, not for the Golden State Warriors' win, but for the He-Man-like performance of James. It wasn't a one-shot performance for the King; instead it will quite possibly go down as the definition of a one-man team—LeBron versus the Warriors. After losing his fellow star teammates Love and Irving to injury, James lugged Cleveland's bench players on his back as he battled his way game after game. He played 275 minutes out of a possible 298 and averaged 38 points, 13.3 rebounds and 8.8 assists. A horde of voices called for LeBron to be named the MVP despite the series loss. It would have made him the first player to be so named since "Mr. Clutch" Jerry West in 1969. James received four of 11 votes, but it wasn't enough to take the award from the hands of the man who won it—Andre Iguodala, who was picked for his work guarding the Cleveland star. Even with the Warriors' small forward pestering him, James became the first player in the history of the NBA Finals to lead both teams in points, rebounds and assists.

That is plain ridiculous.

Despite James' two rings to Jordan's six, he's done the work to be called the best ever.

OVERCOMING ADVERSITY

Greatness and adversity. Combine the two and you get the stuff of legends. When Isiah Thomas scored 43 points, 25 in one quarter, and added 8 assists and 6 steals in the 1988 NBA Finals while hobbling around on one ankle for the Detroit Pistons, it established a modern-day tale of playing through injury.

The injured Willis Reed, right, battles with Wilt Chamberlain in Game 7 of the 1970 NBA Finals. Reed's perseverance through injury to help his Knicks win the title was instantly made legend.

The performance was a throwback to what many call the gutsiest comeback in NBA history. That belongs to Willis Reed, the hulking 6-foot-9, 235-pound center of the 1969–70 New York Knicks. It was LA versus New York in a hotly contested NBA championship that came down to the final game. Reed, who had badly injured his right leg in Game 5 after trying to elude the also-ailing Wilt Chamberlain, missed Game 6, and the Lakers forced the pivotal seventh game back in New York at the fabled Madison Square Garden.

Teammates had implored the injured Reed to give them 20 minutes. But as the warm-ups started, Reed was still in the trainer's room.

"I wanted to play," Reed recalled when recounting the story to NBA.com. "That was the championship . . . I didn't want to have to look at myself in the mirror 20 years later and say that I wished I had tried to play."

Reed also remembers that the needle used for the painkillers was huge, and just the act of administering the medicine caused him a lot of pain.

But as he limped to the floor the Garden fans rose up; the players stopped warm-ups and a tidal wave of appreciative support rained down on Reed and the Knicks.

Dallas Mavericks forward Dirk Nowitzki shoots against the Oklahoma City Thunder during the 2011 Western Conference finals. Nowitzki and Dallas went on to win the NBA title that year.

He didn't throw down many points or hit a buzzer beater. But he was serviceable, keeping Chamberlain to 10 field goals and 2 for 9 in the paint. More telling was the emotional lift it gave his teammates, who ably picked up their center, winning 113–99. It was the Knicks' first-ever title.

Not surprisingly, Michael Jordan added his own power-through-adversity game to the list of the NBA's greatest moments when in 1998 he played in what is known today as "the Flu Game."

The contest is a well-established chronicle—a standout moment from his laundry list of impressive feats.

To recap: It's Game 5 of the NBA Finals and Jordan, who woke up nauseated, dehydrated and fatigued, missed morning practice but donned the jersey come game time. Clearly not himself, Jordan started off slowly but eventually willed himself to drop 30 on the Jazz. With the Bulls victorious, Jordan fell into Scottie Pippen's arms at the end of the game, an enduring image of his exhaustion. They would finish off Utah in Game 6, the sixth and final championship Jordan and the Bulls won. Jordan was named MVP after depositing 39 points to seal the deal. Many thought it was a typical flu, but in 2013, Jordan's former personal trainer would tell the real truth: it was in fact food poisoning the night before the game. A legend was born from a bad pizza ordered late at night in Salt Lake City that did His Airness in. "That was probably the most difficult thing

I've ever done," Jordan would say to NBA.com about the night that became established in NBA lore. It goes down as one of the greatest playoff performances in the history of the NBA.

BUT OVERCOMING ADVERSITY isn't just prevailing when you are physically down and out. It can be stepping up in critical ways when the odds are stacked against you.

On May 13, 2004, not one but two incredible shots occurred back to back in the Western Conference semifinals. After dropping the first two games of the series against the San Antonio Spurs, the LA Lakers stormed back, capped off by their improbable 74–73 Game 5 victory on the road. Derek Fisher's dagger with 0.4 seconds left dispatched the Spurs that evening, and the fact he even got it off with nearly no time remaining was mind-blowing. The fact he actually sunk it established Fisher's rep as a money-ball shooter who rose to the big occasion.

To add to the legend, the unbelievable shot came directly after Tim Duncan hit his own improbable, off-balance 18-footer from the top of the key with Shaquille O'Neal in his face to go ahead by one point. Rare the day it's been when two dying-second shots happen in near synchronicity, and the image of Fisher—running off the court and into the tunnel with a trail of teammates following—is lodged in the collective memory bank of NBA fans.

Bill Russell loops a hook shot over the head of Jim Krebs of the Los Angeles Lakers in the 1962 NBA Finals. Russell and his Boston Celtics took the series in seven games.

Dirk Nowitzki, too, had to overcome adversity to earn the respect he rightfully deserved.

Anyone in the league would let you know that the German is a damn good ball player, but his 48-point performance in the 2011 Western Conference finals versus Oklahoma cemented a long, impressive career. Critics loved to pick apart the mostly hollow theory that the Euro was a choker.

In 2006, the Mavericks made the NBA Finals for the first time in his tenure but lost the championship to the Dwyane Wade–led Miami Heat after leading 2-0. People forget Dirk went off for 50 that year in the West finals versus Phoenix, scoring 22 in the final frame of Game 5. The following season, the Mavericks lost in the first round to eighth seed Golden State—the same year Nowitzki won MVP—the first time a number one seed lost to an eighth. Despite being the most dominant player in the league, with an NBA Finals trip and an MVP nod, it seemed an asterisk always followed Nowitzki.

Until 2011.

Finally given the chance to expunge his critics, the floppy-haired German hoisted a now underdog Mavs team on his back in Game 1 of the 2011 Western Conference finals against the surging Oklahoma Thunder, who boasted Durant, Westbrook and Harden. Dirk sent a message with 48 points on 12-of-15 shooting, including an astronomical 24 of 24 from the line. He missed just three shots the entire night. Dallas silenced Oklahoma over the course of the series, and Nowitzki exacted revenge on the Heat in a rematch of the 2006 finals, defeating another sparkling trio of James, Wade and Bosh. He finally shed the image of a playoff choker and was named NBA Finals MVP. That 48-point night where he barely missed a basket set the tone, and the rest is history.

BIGS PLAYING BIG

Big moments from physically large men. For years, that was almost exclusively what the NBA offered.

Before the widening of the key and the establishment of the three-point line, bigs ruled the roost—sitting under the bucket in

the paint, depositing pick-and-roll plays, or scooping up errant outside jumpers for putbacks.

Players like George Mikan, Bill Walton and Kareem Abdul-Jabbar etched legendary postseason performances. Then, in another stratosphere, is Bill Russell.

Most of us probably don't remember the 1962 NBA Finals, but it featured the two storied franchises in the NBA at the time: the Boston Celtics and Los Angeles Lakers. It pitted east versus west and is the last NBA Finals Game 7 to ever go to overtime. Inside the eventual Celtics series win were two monumental performances. Lakers forward Elgin Baylor put up 61 points (and 22 boards) in Game 5 on the road, a finals record that remains today. (Jordan holds the all-time single-game playoff record with 63 points in 1986, the first glimpse into his superstardom.) Baylor's 33 points in one half

Hakeem Olajuwon climbs the ladder over San Antonio Spurs forward Dennis Rodman for one of his 75 rebounds over the course of the series.

stood for 25 years until Eric "Sleepy" Floyd broke the record in 1987 (more on that later). In Game 7, though, the tables turned.

Bill Russell dominated the game, putting up 30 points and an astronomical mark of 40 rebounds. Russell collected 370 total rebounds in 14 playoff games that season—and in his career that is only his third best playoff showing. His averages of 22.9 points, 27 rebounds, and 5.7 assists sealed the deal for the Celtics, who would go on to win several more rings that decade during their dynasty run. Russell finished his playoff career 10-0 in Game 7s, which says a little something about rising to the occasion.

The Lakers also figured in on many great playoff performances, and one was during the 2000 NBA Finals from the man who was as big as they came. Shaq.

At 7-foot-1 and 325 pounds, the Big Aristotle could dominate, but there's a difference between utter dominance and a quiet, controlled supremacy.

When the Lakers beat the Pacers in the 2000 NBA Finals, Shaquille O'Neal posted a not-so-subtle line of 43 points and 19 rebounds in Game 1. It set the tone for a dominant series that saw O'Neal emerge as the go-to man after 21-year-old Kobe Bryant suffered an ankle injury midway through the series when Jalen Rose stepped on said joint. Shaq finished with no fewer than 33 points in any game, and in Game 6, he dropped 41 points and 12 rebounds against a guard-heavy Pacers team that starred Reggie Miller. O'Neal dominated an aging 7-foot-4 Rik Smits in the paint, and with the Pacers hacking Shaq at every opportunity thanks to his poor free-throwing skills, he made enough from the stripe to seal the win. Hack-a-Shaq has gained in popularity again, most notably in the recent second-round playoff series between the Houston Rockets and Los Angeles Clippers. Both big men, DeAndre Jordan and Dwight Howard, are poor free throwers, and both coaches elected to put the other center on the line, which doesn't exactly make for free-flowing basketball. But it can likely be traced back to that 2000 series when Shaq put the Lakers on his shoulders. It was Shaq, not Kobe, who won that series, inspiring future big men and future NBA coaches alike.

Although he may lack the rings of Shaq, Bryant or Jordan, Hakeem Olajuwon took his Houston Rockets to two titles and posted massive playoff numbers during his career that largely go unnoticed.

In 1987, Hakeem the Dream posted a 49-point, 25-rebound, 6-block night, years before he'd win those back-to-back titles in the

mid-90s. In 1988, while Houston was swept by the Dallas Mavericks, it wasn't due to a lack of effort from Olajuwon. The Houston big averaged 37.5 points and 16.8 rebounds per game.

And what about those back-to-back titles? The Dream put up averages of 28.9 points and 11 rebounds in 1994, and 33 and 10.3 in 1995.

The 1995 Western Conference finals was the stuff of legend for Olajuwon. Facing off against David Robinson, Dennis Rodman and the San Antonio Spurs, the Houston center dominated, putting up 40-plus points in three of the series' six games, and 39 in the final contest. Robinson cracked 30 only once against Houston, and needing a win in Game 6 to stay alive, he mustered only 19 points.

Olajuwon's record-setting PER was set during the lost playoff opportunity against Dallas in 1987, but he kept on working and was eventually rewarded.

The late great Wilt Chamberlain owns a laundry list of NBA playoff records, including most rebounds in one postseason game (41), despite winning the ultimate prize only twice in his career. The man has his own Wikipedia page just for records he's set. If the argument of greatest playoff performers is based solely on titles, however, Wilt's not even in the conversation.

But there's no doubt he was one of the most dominant postseason performers of his era. He led the NBA in playoff rebounds per game in eight of the 13 seasons his teams made the extra session. And in the five seasons he didn't lead the league, he was second.

Even late in his career, working under the rim for the LA Lakers, Chamberlain was effective. He was able to leave the scoring to others, and at 35 on the 1972 Lakers title winners, he averaged a double-double and led the league in rebounds.

THE GREATEST PLAYOFF PERFORMER YOU'VE NEVER HEARD OF

One man dared take on the mighty LA Lakers in the 1987 playoffs. Before the Bulls made their legendary run in the 90s, there was the Magic Johnson–led Lakers, the crème de la crème of the NBA a decade prior to Jordan's reign. Kareem Abdul-Jabbar and James Worthy rounded out an All-Star cast of characters that would lift the trophy that season, their fourth since 1980. The Golden State Warriors had missed the dance for years but surprisingly sent the Utah Jazz home in the first round after staging an improbable comeback after being down 2-0. They won the clinching Game 5 on the road in Salt Lake City. Their second-round prize? A group of goliaths who had already drunk champagne in 1980, 1982 and 1985. But in 1987, one man dared take on those mighty Lakers. Entering Game 4, Golden State had lost three straight, and by a hefty margin. But that night, the Warriors woke up. Or one man did. His name was Sleepy Floyd.

Eric "Sleepy" Floyd averaged just 12.8 points per game over his admirable 14-year career, but one evening stands above the rest. The 1986–87 season was perhaps his most complete—he made the All-Star Game and averaged 18.8 points and 10.3 assists. But down 3-0 that postseason to the Lakers, Sleepy'd had enough. By the time the game finished, Floyd had single-handedly taken down the best squad of NBA players in the league. At one point, he made 12 field goals in a row. He set NBA records that still stand—39 points in one half and 29 in the fourth quarter alone. One writer said following the game: "The hair on my neck was standing. The most incredible feeling I've ever had at a sporting event." The YouTube clip of the highlights is equally goosebump-inducing.

The former Georgetown star finished the game with 51 points, etching himself in the basketball history books with an unimaginable, out-of-nowhere performance. The current Warriors team, with the likes of hot-handed Splash Brothers Steph Curry and Klay Thompson, almost feel like heir apparents to Sleepy's record after their first-place finish in the Western Conference in 2014–15 and their march to the 2015 NBA title. Thompson especially: he set the regular-season record for most points in a quarter, dropping an *en fuego* 37 points in the third quarter versus Sacramento midway through the season, finishing 13 of 13 with nine three-pointers. Perhaps Thompson channeled that epic night of Sleepy Floyd, as now both the regular-season and playoff record for most points in a quarter belong to members of Golden State.

Further, Curry set the playoff record for most threes made, and

Eric Floyd drives to the basket during the fourth quarter of his record-setting 51-point playoff game against the Los Angeles Lakers in 1987.

he did it by the second quarter of Game 3 of the Western Conference finals, eclipsing Reggie Miller's mark of 58. Curry and the Warriors still had five wins to go to claim the championship, and in the two quarters and eight games after he set the mark and the Warriors collected their five wins, Curry added 39 more threes. His new mark of 98 seems assailable by only Thompson and himself.

ALTHOUGH CHAMPIONSHIP RINGS may be a starting and end point for some fans, what should make the most difference is how a player affected the outcome of a game or a series. Not one player can do it all and will a team to a championship—the Charles Barkleys and Reggie Millers of the world will always walk around with naked fingers and broken dreams. LeBron couldn't haul a 2007 Cleveland team on his back, and try as he might in 2015, he couldn't do it then, either. But with half his career now in the rearview mirror, he's a perfect example of someone with a brilliant yet flawed postseason record. He's won, he's lost, and he's dominated at every step of the way. No one should doubt the man's ability to rise to the occasion. There are many different ways to measure success. Character and heart sometimes don't line up with numbers. On other nights, whether Michael's battling the flu or Isiah's fighting a twisted ankle, greatness occurs and enters into the lore of playoff basketball forever.

JOAKIM NOAH

MIAMI HEAT

POSITION CENTER–POWER FORWARD / **SHOOTS** LEFT / **HEIGHT** 6'11" / **WEIGHT** 235 LB. / **DRAFTED** 2003, TORONTO RAPTORS, 4TH OVERALL

CHRIS BOSH [1]

AS THE FOURTH overall pick in the 2003 draft, Chris Bosh belongs to one of the best classes in NBA history—one that includes LeBron James and Dwyane Wade (who would later become teammates with Bosh), as well as Carmelo Anthony. But Bosh carved his own path despite the fanfare surrounding his fellow draftees, proving that slow and steady can win the ultimate prize.

A standout at Lincoln High School, Bosh dominated the Dallas, Texas, scene. His Tigers went 40-0 in his senior year en route to being named the best basketball program in the USA. He played one season of college at Georgia Tech, putting up 15.6 points, 9 rebounds and 2.2 blocks per game, and while his good-naturedness is a trademark now, it belies an uber-competitive nature honed over years competing against his brother Joel. Bosh grew up in awe of center Kevin Garnett, morphing into the same tall, athletic body type as his predecessor. Bosh is also whip-smart and carried a near 4.0 GPA into college.

Playing on such a well-known high school team meant other players received all the accolades, and many pundits felt several of his teammates would make the NBA before Bosh. But soon the star forward's work ethic and attitude eclipsed everyone around him. Although Georgia Tech didn't advance during his only year there, he left the program as a can't-miss top prospect. And yet because of the talent of the 2003 draft, and the fact he went north of the border to the Toronto Raptors, Bosh's arrival in the NBA was relatively low key.

The Raptors, at the end of the Vince Carter era, had potential following their brief playoff run earlier in the decade, but injuries to Carter and Jalen Rose put the Raptors at 33-49 during Bosh's rookie season, where he posted solid numbers (11.5 points and 7.4 rebounds in 63 starts).

Carter was soon traded and Bosh became the centerpiece of the team. Former coach Sam Mitchell said: "For a superstar, he was easy to coach. He wasn't demanding. He wasn't a diva." He'd take Toronto into the postseason twice, but both were early-round exits.

Wearing No. 4 and nicknamed "CB4," Bosh spent seven seasons plying his trade in Toronto, but the lack of postseason success drove him to free agency, and he signed with the Miami Heat in 2010, where he remains today. In Bosh's contract season, he put up career numbers: 24.8 points and 10.8 rebounds while shooting 80 percent from the line. No other player that year averaged 24 and 10.

Bosh is a handful, whether at power forward or center. Possessing a slick midranger and a 7-foot-4 wingspan, the 6-foot-11, 235-pounder is quick, agile and athletic. He can play both big and small ball depending on the matchup. He shifted to center in Miami and added a three-point shot to his arsenal that is next to impossible to guard if you're a big man in the middle on the other side of the ball. As he's aged, his proficiency on pick-and-roll defense, especially against bigger men, has been lauded as one of the best in the NBA.

In leaving Toronto Bosh sacrificed being the guy the ball went through so his team could win. He took criticism after Miami's first finals loss and was called "soft" and a "fake superstar."

Miami won back-to-back titles, however, and Bosh said, en route to that second championship, "I just want to be the type of dude that did everything I could to help my team win."

Bosh had a health scare halfway through 2014–15, when blood clots were discovered in his lungs. The Heat, already without James after he bolted to Cleveland, were struggling. But without Bosh in the frontcourt, it was doubly difficult, and the former NBA champions missed the playoffs. He still averaged 21 points and 7 off the glass in 44 games while shooting 37.5 percent from behind the arc.

Bosh was able to thrive in Miami when

he wasn't forced to shoulder the load, and he was part of a threesome that dominated the NBA for several years. With the addition of Goran Dragic at point guard, it may be Bosh's time to shine if he plays a more traditional pick-and-roll offense. He may be asked one final time to be the man. But it appears he'll do anything, cover anyone, as long as the team wins.

That's the sign of a true professional.

CAREER HIGHLIGHTS

- Named an NBA All-Rookie (First Team) in 2003–04
- Has played in 10 All-Star Games (2006–2015)
- Is a three-time NBA Shooting Stars champion (2013–2015)
- Won an Olympic gold medal with the U.S. men's basketball team in Beijing in 2008
- Is the Toronto Raptors' all-time leading scorer

POSITION CENTER / **SHOOTS** RIGHT / **HEIGHT** 7'1" / **WEIGHT** 265 LB. / **DRAFTED** 2007, LOS ANGELES LAKERS, 48TH OVERALL

MARC GASOL ³³

MARC GASOL WAS always good—but he was also the younger brother of star NBA player Pau, he of two championship rings with the Los Angeles Lakers. It's taken several years to establish himself among the NBA's elite, but the younger Gasol is finally making his own mark, and the Memphis Grizzlies have soared to the top of the Western Conference thanks to his emphatic season in 2014–15.

Gasol's early life was spent in Spain, but by the time Pau had been drafted by Memphis, the Gasols had moved to Germantown, Tennessee. Marc played his final two years of high school ball in the Memphis area before returning to his home country to further his craft in the Liga ACB while Pau plied his trade in the association. That time in Spain paid off in spades—Marc was named Spanish League MVP in 2008—and the Lakers drafted the center late in the second round in 2007. His rights were traded later that year—for his brother Pau, in fact, who played seven years in Memphis—and Marc has since become the cornerstone of a Grizzlies squad that at times challenged for best NBA team in 2014–15. Much of that success has fallen on the 7-foot-1 shoulders of Gasol, whose emergence as one of the most consistent centers in the game hasn't gone unnoticed.

Marc's always had some serious shoes to fill—his brother was Rookie of the Year and alongside Kobe Bryant dominated the league, winning two championships. And Marc's weight was always an issue. Not so in 2014–15—his teammate Mike Conley, upon seeing Gasol compete in the FIBA championships in the summer of 2014, barely recognized his center. "It look[ed] like he lost 50 pounds," Conley remarked early in the season about the former Defensive Player of the Year in 2012–13. That season, he hauled down 7.8 rebounds

CAREER HIGHLIGHTS

- Named NBA Defensive Player of the Year for 2012–13
- Has played in two All-Star Games (2012, 2015)
- Was an All-NBA First Team selection for 2014–15
- Won an Olympic silver medal with the Spanish men's basketball team in Beijing in 2008 and London in 2012
- Finished second in assists per game by a center in 2014–15 (3.8)

and had 1.7 blocks playing center for the league's best defensive team, while setting career highs in free-throw percentage at .848 and leading all centers in assists with 318. He'd become an integral part of the Grizzlies, and when he was sidelined the following season for 23 games with a knee injury, the team suffered without him in the lineup.

What he needed to add to his game was offense. The weight loss entering the 2014–15 season immediately made him a scoring threat from beyond the paint, and the combo of deft touch from the 20-foot range with a body big enough to bang inside is lethal. It's also allowed him to hang longer in tough physical games. "You don't have to take the co-pilot seat and let somebody else take over," Gasol said in November. Case in point: his 26-point, 7-rebound and 9-assist performance against fellow big LaMarcus Aldridge and the Portland Trail Blazers at the start of the year, or his 30 points, 6 boards and 6 assists versus the Dirk Nowitzki–led Dallas Mavericks the following week. Other highlights included 6 blocks against Charlotte; the outrageous line of 12 points, 16 rebounds, 8 assists,

2 blocks and 3 steals versus Orlando; and his career-high 33 points in the final game of the season.

Marc joined Pau as a 2015 All-Star starter, making them the first siblings to achieve the feat in NBA history. It was for good reason—Marc's statistics overall that year were off the chart. He finished second in assists for his position behind Joakim Noah, with 3.8 dimes per game, and third in scoring for centers with 17.4 points, adding 7.8 rebounds for good measure. He hit 80 percent from the stripe and averaged nearly 1.6 blocks per game while accumulating 20 double-doubles over the course of the season, in which he played 81 games and the fourth-most minutes of any NBA center.

But it's the intangibles he provides on the court that have truly helped Memphis excel. Whether he's dropping turnaround jumpers or boxing out other big men on the defensive end, Gasol's game has flourished in all facets, and with rebounding machine Zach Randolph beside him in the frontcourt, the Grizz have a dangerous one-two punch up front. They admirably lost in the second round to the eventual

champion Golden State Warriors, but it wasn't due to lack of effort on Gasol's part, who averaged 20 and 10 over 11 playoff games.

At 30, trimmer and faster than ever before, Gasol is undeniably one of the best two-way centers in the game today. Edging into his prime NBA years thanks to several seasons in Europe, the man in the middle will be seeking his own ring to wear alongside his brother's hardware. He's certainly making a case, not only to supplant Pau as one of the most effective international centers in the NBA today, but as one of its best centers, period.

POSITION CENTER–POWER FORWARD / **SHOOTS** RIGHT / **HEIGHT** 6'11" / **WEIGHT** 275 LB. / **DRAFTED** 2004, ORLANDO MAGIC, 1ST OVERALL

DWIGHT HOWARD 12

DWIGHT HOWARD MIGHT be a polarizing personality, but his talent is unmistakable. And although he plays the game differently than most, the Houston Rockets center is an NBA star whose tenure has been impressive in more ways than one.

With a wingspan that stretches across the paint, Howard opted to skip college and try his chances in the pros as a 6-foot-11, 18-year-old out of high school, one of the last high schoolers to join the NBA. His physicality was so promising that he was the third high schooler (after Kwame Brown, 2001, and LeBron James, 2003) to be selected first overall when Orlando picked him in 2004. He made an immediate impression during his rookie season, averaging 12 points and 10 boards and starting all 82 games for the Magic.

Howard quickly turned into an A-plus guy on the back end, causing havoc for opposing players with his length, arm span and efficiency off the glass. Currently ranked 12th all-time in rebounds per game behind Dennis Rodman and ahead of Kareem Abdul-Jabbar, he has led the NBA five times during his career, and in his final year with Orlando (2011–12), he hauled down a career-best 14.5 rebounds. He was named Defensive Player of the Year for three consecutive seasons starting in 2008–09 and five times has been named to the All-NBA First Team.

When he donned a Superman T-shirt and cape at the 2008 All-Star Game, it showed the goofy, playful side of one of the NBA's elite big men, and he won the Slam Dunk Contest because of his inventiveness. Although it may have endeared him to the fans, his rep on the court remained in sharp contrast, often cited as a respect issue among players.

The perceived rift between him and Kobe Bryant largely overshadowed his year with the LA Lakers in 2012–13 (a team that traded for him to help bring a championship back to Los Angeles). And while Kevin Durant was injured at the beginning of the 2014–15 season, the usually docile Oklahoma Thunder star got up off the bench to bark at Howard. Former player-turned-analyst and legendary trash-talker Gary Payton said in 2014 that Howard "gets on people's nerves."

This is the same center, mind you, who took the Magic to the NBA Finals in 2009, their first time back at the dance since the Magic finished runner-up in 1994–95 on the prowess of another big, Shaquille O'Neal. Howard's run saw the Magic defeat the defending champion Boston Celtics, led up front by Howard's idol, Kevin Garnett. In Game 6 alone, Howard put up a gargantuan 23 points and 22 boards. He and the Magic then quickly disposed of LeBron James and the first-place Cleveland Cavaliers. In the final game of that series, Howard put up an incredible 40 points and 14 rebounds. Say what you will about his temperament, he got it done—and yet largely he's been criticized for a personality that doesn't mesh with other players.

He joined James Harden and the Houston Rockets in 2014–15 in their bid to take over the Western Conference. It was a fresh start for the mercurial center with the effusive smile. Too often thrust into the spotlight for reasons unrelated to his on-court performance, Houston proved that Howard can share the spotlight—something Lakers fans claim he was incapable of doing in LA.

One thing about Howard that's not up for debate is his terrible free-throw shooting. The 275-pound center hasn't cracked 60 percent from the charity stripe in any season since his rookie year. But he makes up for it in minutes played, gobbling up 35-plus a night his entire career. And until 2014–15, when he missed 41 games with a knee injury, he'd missed only 52 games over 10 seasons, which highlights his remarkable conditioning. One need only ask his former backup in Orlando, the rising Polish star Marcin Gortat, to know that Howard's practices were as hard as his games.

Maybe he's just the guy people love to hate, a scapegoat in the soap opera behind the scenes in the NBA. No one denies the immense talent on the court and the next-level defense he brings to a team. With a new future in Houston, Howard will silence his critics if he can bring a championship to Texas. Maybe that will take the target off the back of one of the league's greatest centers.

CAREER HIGHLIGHTS

- Named an NBA All-Rookie (First Team) in 2004–05
- Named NBA Defensive Player of the Year three times (2008–09 to 2010–11)
- Has played in eight All-Star Games (2007–2014)
- Won the NBA Slam Dunk Contest in 2008
- Is the all-time leading scorer in Orlando

POSITION CENTER–POWER FORWARD / **SHOOTS** RIGHT / **HEIGHT** 6'10" / **WEIGHT** 290 LB. / **DRAFTED** 2004, BOSTON CELTICS, 15TH OVERALL

AL JEFFERSON 25

AL JEFFERSON JUST goes about his business. He's been doing it for years. He's never been an All-Star. He's never been named a first- or second-team All-NBA player, and he's never made it to the NBA Finals. But the prodigious center has been one of the most consistent players in the league—and criminally underrated, some would say.

Jefferson was such a stud at a young age that he skipped college altogether, opting for the draft right out of high school, one of the last men in the association to do so. He was a beast during his senior year at Prentiss High in Mississippi, where he scored 42.6 points on average and dragged down 18 boards before landing on the cover of SLAM magazine beside future stars Dwight Howard and Josh Smith. Despite a scholarship offer from Arkansas, an invitation to Michael Jordan's summer camp before his final year of high school— along with an alley-oop finish from His Airness himself—changed Jefferson's mind about going to college.

He was going to the NBA.

Drafted 15th overall by the Boston Celtics in 2004, he played three years in Beantown before being shipped off to Minnesota in the blockbuster Kevin Garnett deal. There Jefferson earned a five-year, $65 million contract in 2008, and he repaid the Timberwolves by setting career highs in points per game (23.1) while collecting his third straight season of 11 rebounds or more. He was one of the best young power forwards in the league, the centerpiece of the Minnesota offense, adequately taking over for the revered Garnett.

"Al had never touched the ball that many times in his basketball life," coach Randy Wittman said. "And he liked it."

But after three years, he was again traded thanks to the emergence of another big man in the Timberwolves organization, Kevin Love. This time Big Al was on the move to the Utah Jazz, where he played big minutes and made big contributions in 82 games, posting 37 double-doubles and leading the Jazz to the playoffs. Too bad they caught the San Antonio Spurs as their matchup. Utah lost the series, but Jefferson's averages of 18.3 points and 8.3 rebounds versus Tim Duncan made heads turn.

With his contract up and Utah rebuilding, he signed with the Hornets in 2013 after heavy courting from the Charlotte brass and star guard Kemba Walker, the ninth overall pick of the 2011 draft. Jefferson chose Charlotte because it speaks to his small-town roots in the south, and he has formed a nice two-headed monster with Walker, another player who tends to get overlooked.

At 6-foot-10 and 290 pounds, Jefferson is a load to deal with and a tough matchup even for taller bigs. Late in the 2013–14 season, he was named Eastern Conference Player of the Week, and the Hornets—who'd finished the lockout-shortened 2012–13 season 7-59—were relevant again, finishing 43-39 and making the playoffs.

Jefferson put up 16.6 points per game in 2014–15, adding 8.4 rebounds and just over a block per contest. He started off November in scintillating fashion, averaging more than 20 a night. He contributed 17 points and 16 boards in an early 2015 game against the reigning-champion Spurs. In a March victory versus the lowly LA Lakers, the center posted 21 and 16 on 9-of-19 shooting. Later, against a couple of the Washington Wizards' giants, Jefferson did all he could as the Hornets pushed for the playoffs. He deposited 31 points against Marcin Gortat and Nene and added 10 off

the glass in a 110–107 double OT loss. But his near heroics came at a price, and he finished the last few games on the bench because of injury. The hole in the lineup left the Hornets short, and they finished out of the playoff picture.

At 30 years old, Jefferson is entering the last few meaningful years of his career. Although ankle issues and an ACL tear have hampered him at times, the big man can still put up big points and a big-money effort. He's never had a breakout season—and he probably won't at this stage. But the Hornets are turning the franchise around, and he'll likely be a big piece of the puzzle. One thing is for certain: there's still a final chapter for the big man with the workmanlike attitude.

He certainly deserves a good ending.

CAREER HIGHLIGHTS

- Named an NBA All-Rookie (Second Team) for 2004–05
- Was an All-NBA Third Team selection for 2013–14
- Finished fifth in scoring for centers (16.6) in 2014–15
- Finished 12th in rebounding for centers (8.4) in 2014–15
- Is a seven-time NBA Player of the Week and two-time NBA Player of the Month

SAN ANTONIO SPURS

POSITION SMALL FORWARD / **SHOOTS** RIGHT / **HEIGHT** 6'7" / **WEIGHT** 230 LB. / **DRAFTED** 2011, INDIANA PACERS, 15TH OVERALL

KAWHI LEONARD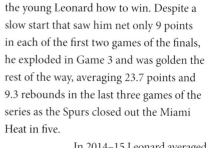

KAWHI LEONARD BARELY registered on the radar two seasons ago. Now, he's one of the most invaluable players for the San Antonio Spurs. In that short time, he was named the MVP of the 2014 NBA Finals and the league's best defensive player the following year.

He's an unassuming 6-foot-7, if that's even possible. The 15th overall pick in the 2011 draft, Leonard was traded by the Indiana Pacers to San Antonio, where he's been a revelation; his being plucked by the Spurs is another moment of talent evaluation by the franchise that has paid great dividends.

Leonard's two years at San Diego State were solid, and in his second and final season, the shooting guard took the Aztecs all the way to the Sweet 16. That season he threw up averages of 15.9 points and 10.6 rebounds. But Leonard hasn't had the easiest route. His father was killed outside the car wash he owned in Compton in 2008 while Kawhi was in high school. Leonard grew up there washing cars and learned a work ethic that transferred to the court. The tragedy instilled a quiet toughness in his personality, and his agent called Leonard "the most dedicated guy I've ever been around."

En route to his first championship and first finals MVP award, Leonard contributed 12.8 points and 6.2 boards to the Spurs' attack during the regular season. His presence rounded out a formidably deep group intent on proving that age ain't nothin' but a number—with veterans like Tim Duncan, Tony Parker and Manu Ginobili showing

the young Leonard how to win. Despite a slow start that saw him net only 9 points in each of the first two games of the finals, he exploded in Game 3 and was golden the rest of the way, averaging 23.7 points and 9.3 rebounds in the last three games of the series as the Spurs closed out the Miami Heat in five.

In 2014–15 Leonard averaged 16.5 points, 7.2 rebounds and 2.5 assists in 31.8 minutes per game despite missing 18 games in December and January to injury. Basically, he's been the engine of the team, filling in for the aging trio of Spurs superstars when needed. He's a presence on both ends of the floor, and his point production increased by four per game over the previous season even as he was named the best defensive player in the league. But perhaps because he's the young gun on a team of All-Stars, Leonard's contributions are still overlooked. Or perhaps it's his low-key personality and humility, especially since the loss of his father. Perseverance is a word that comes up over and over again whenever someone mentions the 23-year-old star.

What's clear: The Spurs are Leonard's team going forward.

CAREER HIGHLIGHTS

- Named MVP of the NBA Finals for 2013–14
- Named NBA Defensive Player of the Year for 2014–15
- Named an NBA All-Rookie (First Team) in 2011–12
- Named to NBA All-Defensive First Team in 2014–15
- Led the league in steals per game in 2014–15 (2.3)

The international trifecta that nurtured him will soon be sailing into the sunset, and the shooting guard will be called on to carry the team even more than he'd done in 2014–15. Midway through that season, Leonard added 15 rebounds to 17 points in a win versus the Denver Nuggets. Twice in March he had 5 steals during a game, and he was unstoppable that month at the other end, averaging 19.3 points per contest and 7.3 boards. Nine times that month he had 20 points or more, and he finished the season with 14 double-doubles, a career high.

But where he really excels is in shutting down the opponent's top players—making long nights out of games for the league's top stars. He led the league in steals, and he's simply too much of everything all at once. He's too big for some, too long for others, too quick for many and too tenacious on and off the ball for most. (His hands are also massive, 11.25 inches from pinkie to thumb, more than 50 percent larger than the average person and reminiscent of another top defender, Hall of Famer Scottie Pippen.)

The Spurs—despite five championships since 1999—have never registered back-to-back titles. In 2014–15 the team bowed out in seven games to the LA Clippers. If they want to get back to the head of the pack, they'll need Leonard to rise to the occasion the next time they make the postseason. He's only 23, but with the wisdom passed on from the NBA's elder statesmen, he'll be ready.

Just wait.

TORONTO RAPTORS

POSITION POINT GUARD / **SHOOTS** RIGHT / **HEIGHT** 6'0" / **WEIGHT** 205 LB. / **DRAFTED** 2006, MEMPHIS GRIZZLIES, 24TH OVERALL

KYLE LOWRY 7

KYLE LOWRY GETS no respect. No respect for his talent. No respect for being a leader. No respect for being a team guy. Or maybe he does and he's just had us all fooled.

Since arriving in Toronto and being thrust into the starting point guard role, the feisty 6-footer has proven everyone wrong. He's got all the talent in the world and has morphed into the heart and soul of the franchise. Above all, he's shown the basketball world he's willing to sacrifice everything for the win.

The Philadelphia native was drafted 24th overall in the 2006 draft by Memphis after just two years at Villanova, where in his final year he tallied 11 points, 3.7 assists and 2.3 steals per game. Villanova, a suburban school in a wealthy part of Philadelphia, appeared to be an odd fit for Lowry. But after being passed over by several high-profile teams like Xavier and North Carolina, the hardscrabble city boy whose father had abandoned him and his brother when he was just 8 years old, stayed close to home and far away all at once. Alvin Williams, former NBA player and coach at Villanova, described Lowry as "a stubborn, hardnosed kid." When his father left, Lowry developed trust issues that permeated his game. But 'Nova needed someone exactly with his skill set: a guard unafraid to drive to the hoop and to give them a much-needed edge in the backcourt—things he's still doing in the NBA.

A blown ACL early in his freshman year curtailed his attitude, and Lowry adjusted. By sophomore year, he helped earn a number one seed for Villanova. They lost in the Elite Eight to Florida, and Lowry declared for the NBA. He didn't last long in Memphis, just two seasons, where he was branded a me-first guy, a reputation that's taken years to shake.

No one has ever doubted his physical gifts—built like a Mack truck but blessed with the foot speed of a gazelle. He spent his early years splitting time with other point guards in Memphis and Houston, skilled players like Mike Conley Jr., Goran Dragic and Aaron Brooks. It's Lowry's head they questioned, not his heart—what was in between the ears is what coaches wondered about. He also had a problem staying healthy due to his hardnosed style of play, injuring his wrist 10 games into his rookie season and undergoing sports hernia surgery later with Houston, a by-product of his take-no-prisoners, foul-me-if-you-want attitude.

But he began to flourish in Houston, starting 71 games in 2010–11. The two previous seasons he had started exactly zero. Not surprisingly he posted career bests. But after contracting a bacterial infection, he missed time again and was moved to the Toronto Raptors for Gary Forbes and a first-rounder. It wasn't a rosy beginning. The Raps still had Jose Calderon, an established pure point guard. Lowry wasn't pleased with being a backup. So he sulked. A meeting with Raptors general manager Masai Ujiri on the day before training camp transformed the once-stubborn guard into a different man, and he played like it in 2013–14, lifting the Raptors to the playoffs with career highs in points (17.9), assists (7.4), rebounds (4.7), three-point percentage (38 percent) and minutes played.

The Raptors gutted it out against the Brooklyn Nets that season in the playoffs, taking it to a seventh and final game, with Lowry tasked with the final, game-winning shot. He missed. It stung. But it served notice to the NBA—the Raptors were no joke, and this was Lowry's team, live or die. Paul Pierce, after the game, passed Lowry in the hall and called him "an animal."

He subsequently signed a four-year, $48 million deal to stay north of the border and owned the role of emotional heartbeat for the franchise during the 2014–15 season, in which he was named a starter in the NBA All-Star Game. Among point guards, he's been hanging with the leaders in assist-to-turnover ratio and consistently changed

CAREER HIGHLIGHTS

the outcomes of games with his defensive tenacity and timely steals. "It's just the DNA of Kyle," coach Dwane Casey says of his defensive prowess.

The success of a franchise rests in the palms of a once-disgruntled point guard who finally learned to trust his coaches, his teammates and ultimately himself. And it appears everyone, fans included, have trusted him back.

- Drafted by the Memphis Grizzlies in the first round (24th overall) in 2006
- Played in the 2015 NBA All-Star Game
- Named NBA Player of the Month for December 2014
- Is a two-time NBA Player of the Week
- Is the Raptors' all-time leader in triple-doubles

POSITION CENTER–POWER FORWARD / **SHOOTS** RIGHT / **HEIGHT** 6'11" / **WEIGHT** 232 LB. / **DRAFTED** 2007, CHICAGO BULLS, 9TH OVERALL

JOAKIM NOAH 13

WITH HIS SCRAGGLY beard and ponytail, Joakim Noah could easily be mistaken for a Brooklyn hipster when, in fact, he's one of the NBA's best defenders. Noah is a cornerstone of the Chicago Bulls franchise—the heart and soul of the Derrick Rose–led bunch who scratches and claws to get wins, proving time and time again that he belongs among the elite of the NBA.

Just how good a season did the Bulls center have in 2013–14? He finished fourth in MVP voting, behind the likes of LeBron James and Kevin Durant.

His ascent toward the top of the NBA heap came on the heels of a stellar 2012–13 campaign, where Noah joined the likes of Hakeem Olajuwon and Shaquille O'Neal in an elite category of men who've gone 20-20-10, after he blocked 11 shots while adding 23 points and 21 rebounds against the Philadelphia 76ers. He was an All-Star that year and again in 2013–14.

Most impressively, Noah was named the Defensive Player of the Year in 2013–14. He accepted the honor on the strength of per-game averages of 12.6 points, 11.3 boards, 5.4 assists, 1.5 blocks and 1.2 steals. He even dished 14 assists in one game versus

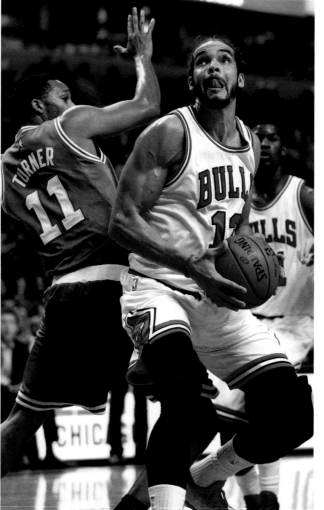

the Knicks en route to a triple-double, the most helpers by a center since 1986.

Noah had to be that good for the Bulls, as former league MVP Rose missed significant time with knee injuries in 2012–13 and 2013–14. Even still, his career years weren't enough to single-handedly lift the Bulls, and they bowed out of the playoffs early.

Beyond the numbers, it's Noah's tenaciousness and will to win that make him such a valuable commodity. He was a standout at the University of Florida, helping lead the school to back-to-back NCAA championships alongside future NBA stars Al Horford and Corey Brewer. All three would be drafted in the top 10 in 2007, with Noah going ninth to the Bulls.

The forward comes from athletic pedigree, the son of French tennis star Yannick Noah, the 1983 French Open winner. His grandfather played soccer for the Cameroon national team. But Noah, upon moving to the United States when he was 13, fell in love with hoops. One of his coaches from his time playing in New York's Hell's Kitchen said, "I knew [Noah] would go pro when he was 14 years old," citing a work ethic that included staying in the gym after school until midnight. As Noah progressed, his hustle for loose balls and attention to defense drew praise from his coaches, who used him as an example of how to play.

But the enigmatic athlete had a quiet freshman year at Florida, playing just nine

minutes a game. A stern talking to and an attention to fitness sparked Noah, and he began to eat up the SEC. In one game during his sophomore year, he went off for 37 points. In the NCAA championship game, he posted 16 points, 9 rebounds and 6 blocked shots—a line like that on the biggest collegiate stage in the nation is something special.

The 2014–15 season saw the return of Rose from injury (mostly) as well as the addition of pure center Pau Gasol. The new addition meant Noah moved from center to power forward, where his averages are down but his impact is not. At 6-foot-11 and 232 pounds, he cuts an imposing figure, a deadly mix of size, speed and dexterity that drives opponents nuts. With Gasol on board, the one-two punch up front for the Bulls is hard to

play against, and while Noah has settled into double-double territory most nights, his 30-plus minutes on the court every game is difficult to replace. Versus Boston in November, he put up 15 points, 14 rebounds, 6 assists and 6 blocks. Against Golden State in January, he went for 18 points and 15 rebounds, 6 assists and 2 steals.

Quite simply, Noah does it all, and if there is one term to define him, it's heart and soul. That's who Noah was in high school and college, and that's who he is now in the NBA. He rarely takes a play off and never gets enough credit for doing the little things that make his team better. He's vocal, intense and always in the mix. He's a little bit wild, but that's what has always made him effective—and what the Bulls hope will make their team a winner.

CAREER HIGHLIGHTS

- Named NBA Defensive Player of the Year for 2013–14
- Named to NBA All-Defensive First Team twice (2012–13, 2013–14)
- Was an All-NBA First Team selection for 2013–14
- Has played in two All-Star Games (2013, 2014)
- Led all NBA centers in assists per game (4.7) in 2014–15

MEMPHIS GRIZZLIES

POSITION POWER FORWARD–CENTER / **SHOOTS** LEFT / **HEIGHT** 6'9" / **WEIGHT** 260 LB. / **DRAFTED** 2001, PORTLAND TRAIL BLAZERS, 19TH OVERALL

ZACH RANDOLPH 50

SOME MEN ARE born to bang the glass, born to sit under the rim and bang big bodies and haul down the rock. It may not be the most glamorous job in the NBA, but ever since the likes of Charles Barkley and Dennis Rodman made rebounding fashionable, we've been graced with men like Zach Randolph.

As a freshman at Marion High School in Indiana, he started for the varsity team—a rarity in the basketball-mad state. As a senior he took the Giants to the state championship. He could have leapt straight from high school to the NBA if it weren't for a rule change that now requires athletes to play a minimum of one year of basketball after high school.

Randolph landed at Michigan State in 2000, where in just 20 minutes per game, he put up 10.8 points and 6.7 rebounds for the Spartans—then he opted for the NBA, and he was drafted 19th overall in 2001 by the Portland Trail Blazers. Randolph spent six seasons out west with the "Jail Blazers," a team that played above the law on and off the court. His name showed up on the police blotter along with many other teammates, but ultimately he was never charged with anything and emerged as a valuable power forward, signing a six-year, $84 million contract in 2004. He put up averages of 23.6 points and 10.1 rebounds per game in 2006–07. But the big contract was too much for Portland to swallow, and they traded Randolph in 2007 to the New York

Knicks for Steve Francis in order to make room for that year's number one pick, Greg Oden. Unfortunately for the Trail Blazers, Oden was the biggest bust of the past decade. "Z-Bo," on the other hand, grabbed a career-high 12.5 boards per

game for New York before he was dealt to the Clippers in 2008.

Another deal landed Randolph in Memphis in 2009, and this time, he's stuck around, establishing himself over the past six seasons as one of the biggest inside presences in the NBA. He's twice made the All-Star Team, and his work under the rim has helped turn the Grizzlies from also-rans to playoff contenders.

For much of the 2014–15 season, the Grizz spent time atop the Western Conference, finishing 55-27 and second in the Southwest Division. Randolph, for his part, is just doing what he always does. With his trademark headband and left-handed post moves, the 6-foot-9, 260-pound forward has formed a formidable pair up front with center Marc Gasol. Case in point: in early January, with Gasol struggling early from the field versus Phoenix, Randolph scored 27 points and added 17 boards, while Gasol scored the crucial baskets down the stretch in a double OT win. There was more to come from Z-Bo: 17 and 22 versus the Detroit Pistons in November, and 18 and 18 against the Toronto Raptors two games later. In a thrilling triple OT victory versus the reigning-champion San Antonio Spurs, Randolph had a monster 21 points and 21 rebounds.

It's hard to say what makes the Indiana native effective. He isn't a great leaper, or necessarily that long. He has small hands for a big man. But in the stocky mold of Barkley, he's big, he's bad and he creates angles to the hoop that allow him to seemingly haul down boards at will. He's quite simply a throwback to the old days: a thick, mean dude in the post who gets to the basket one way or another. He's someone who, as an assistant coach in Portland once said, "has a natural feel for the game."

It wasn't always easy for Randolph. He grew up poor and spent 30 days in juvenile detention for shoplifting jeans because he had only one pair. He missed his entire junior season of high school for possession of stolen guns. But his talent was unmistakable, and his high school coach said in 2012: "I never had a problem once with Zach. We worked hours and hours on that jab step, pull back and shoot the jumper, that little-left handed hook and all the post moves."

He's not likely going to be a Hall of Famer or an MVP. He's often overlooked in favor of the flashy guards and grade-A centers on his teams. But make no mistake—for a franchise to have a player like Randolph in their frontcourt is a blessing, because players willing to grind under the rim the way Randolph does are hard to come by. And generally, they help make the difference between winning and losing.

CAREER HIGHLIGHTS

- Named NBA Most Improved Player for 2003–04
- Has played in two All-Star Games (2010, 2013)
- Was an All-NBA Third Team selection for 2010–11
- Finished seventh in NBA rebounding (10.5) in 2014–15
- Is a four-time NBA Player of the Week

NBA REGULAR SEASON MVP WINNERS

2014-15: Stephen Curry, Golden State Warriors

2013-14: Kevin Durant, Oklahoma City Thunder

2012-13: LeBron James, Miami Heat

2011-12: LeBron James, Miami Heat

2010-11: Derrick Rose, Chicago Bulls

2009-10: LeBron James, Cleveland Cavaliers

2008-09: LeBron James, Cleveland Cavaliers

2007-08: Kobe Bryant, Los Angeles Lakers

2006-07: Dirk Nowitzki, Dallas Mavericks

2005-06: Steve Nash, Phoenix Suns

2004-05: Steve Nash, Phoenix Suns

2003-04: Kevin Garnett, Minnesota Timberwolves

2002-03: Tim Duncan, San Antonio Spurs

2001-02: Tim Duncan, San Antonio Spurs

2000-01: Allen Iverson, Philadelphia 76ers

1999-00: Shaquille O'Neal, Los Angeles Lakers

1998-99: Karl Malone, Utah Jazz

1997-98: Michael Jordan, Chicago Bulls

1996-97: Karl Malone, Utah Jazz

1995-96: Michael Jordan, Chicago Bulls

1994-95: David Robinson, San Antonio Spurs

1993-94: Hakeem Olajuwon, Houston Rockets

1992-93: Charles Barkley, Phoenix Suns

1991-92: Michael Jordan, Chicago Bulls

1990-91: Michael Jordan, Chicago Bulls

1989-90: Earvin Johnson, Los Angeles Lakers

1988-89: Earvin Johnson, Los Angeles Lakers

1987-88: Michael Jordan, Chicago Bulls

1986-87: Earvin Johnson, Los Angeles Lakers

1985-86: Larry Bird, Boston Celtics

1984-85: Larry Bird, Boston Celtics

1983-84: Larry Bird, Boston Celtics

1982-83: Moses Malone, Philadelphia 76ers

1981-82: Moses Malone, Houston Rockets

1980-81: Julius Erving, Philadelphia 76ers

1979-80: Kareem Abdul-Jabbar, Los Angeles Lakers

1978-79: Moses Malone, Houston Rockets

1977-78: Bill Walton, Portland Trail Blazers

1976-77: Kareem Abdul-Jabbar, Los Angeles Lakers

1975-76: Kareem Abdul-Jabbar, Los Angeles Lakers

1974-75: Bob McAdoo, Buffalo Braves

1973-74: Kareem Abdul-Jabbar, Milwaukee Bucks

1972-73: Dave Cowens, Boston Celtics

1971-72: Kareem Abdul-Jabbar, Milwaukee Bucks

1970-71: Kareem Abdul-Jabbar, Milwaukee Bucks

1969-70: Willis Reed, New York Knicks

1968-69: Wes Unseld, Baltimore Bullets

1967-68: Wilt Chamberlain, Philadelphia 76ers

1966-67: Wilt Chamberlain, Philadelphia 76ers

1965-66: Wilt Chamberlain, Philadelphia 76ers

1964-65: Bill Russell, Boston Celtics

1963-64: Oscar Robertson, Cincinnati Royals

1962-63: Bill Russell, Boston Celtics

1961-62: Bill Russell, Boston Celtics

1960-61: Bill Russell, Boston Celtics

1959-60: Wilt Chamberlain, Philadelphia Warriors

1958-59: Bob Pettit, St. Louis Hawks

1957-58: Bill Russell, Boston Celtics

1956-57: Bob Cousy, Boston Celtics

1955-56: Bob Pettit, St. Louis Hawks

KAREEM ABDUL-JABBAR

NBA ALL-STAR GAME MVP WINNERS

2014-15: Russell Westbrook,
Oklahoma City Thunder

2013-14: Kyrie Irving,
Cleveland Cavaliers

2012-13: Chris Paul,
Los Angeles Clippers

2011-12: Kevin Durant,
Oklahoma City Thunder

2010-11: Kobe Bryant,
Los Angeles Lakers

2009-10: Dwyane Wade,
Miami Heat

2008-09: Shaquille O'Neal,
Phoenix Suns (Tie)

2008-09: Kobe Bryant,
Los Angeles Lakers (Tie)

2007-08: LeBron James,
Cleveland Cavaliers

2006-07: Kobe Bryant,
Los Angeles Lakers

2005-06: LeBron James,
Cleveland Cavaliers

2004-05: Allen Iverson,
Philadelphia 76ers

2003-04: Shaquille O'Neal,
Los Angeles Lakers

2002-03: Kevin Garnett,
Minnesota Timberwolves

2001-02: Kobe Bryant,
Los Angeles Lakers

2000-01: Allen Iverson,
Philadelphia 76ers

1999-00: Shaquille O'Neal,
Los Angeles Lakers (Tie)

1999-00: Tim Duncan,
San Antonio Spurs (Tie)

1997-98: Michael Jordan,
Chicago Bulls

1996-97: Glen Rice,
Charlotte Hornets

1995-96: Michael Jordan,
Chicago Bulls

1994-95: Mitch Richmond,
Sacramento Kings

1993-94: Scottie Pippen,
Chicago Bulls

1992-93: John Stockton,
Utah Jazz (Tie)

1992-93: Karl Malone,
Utah Jazz (Tie)

1991-92: Earvin Johnson,
Los Angeles Lakers

1990-91: Charles Barkley,
Philadelphia 76ers

1989-90: Earvin Johnson,
Los Angeles Lakers

1988-89: Karl Malone,
Utah Jazz

1987-88: Michael Jordan,
Chicago Bulls

1986-87: Tom Chambers,
Seattle SuperSonics

1985-86: Isiah Thomas,
Detroit Pistons

1984-85: Ralph Sampson,
Houston Rockets

1983-84: Isiah Thomas,
Detroit Pistons

1982-83: Julius Erving,
Philadelphia 76ers

1981-82: Larry Bird,
Boston Celtics

1980-81: Nate Archibald,
Boston Celtics

1979-80: George Gervin,
San Antonio Spurs

1978-79: David Thompson,
Denver Nuggets

1977-78: Randy Smith,
Buffalo Braves

1976-77: Julius Erving,
Philadelphia 76ers

1975-76: Dave Bing,
Washington Bullets

1974-75: Walt Frazier,
New York Knicks

1973-74: Bob Lanier,
Detroit Pistons

1972-73: Dave Cowens,
Boston Celtics

1971-72: Jerry West,
Los Angeles Lakers

1970-71: Lenny Wilkens,
Seattle SuperSonics

1969-70: Willis Reed,
New York Knicks

1968-69: Oscar Robertson,
Cincinnati Royals

1967-68: Hal Greer,
Philadelphia 76ers

1966-67: Rick Barry,
San Francisco Warriors

1965-66: Adrian Smith,
Cincinnati Royals

1964-65: Jerry Lucas,
Cincinnati Royals

1963-64: Oscar Robertson,
Cincinnati Royals

1962-63: Bill Russell,
Boston Celtics

1961-62: Bob Pettit,
St. Louis Hawks

1960-61: Oscar Robertson,
Cincinnati Royals

1959-60: Wilt Chamberlain,
Philadelphia Warriors

1958-59: Bob Pettit,
St. Louis Hawks (Tie)

1958-59: Elgin Baylor,
Minneapolis Lakers (Tie)

MICHAEL JORDAN

1957-58: Bob Pettit,
St. Louis Hawks

1956-57: Bob Cousy,
Boston Celtics

1955-56: Bob Pettit,
St. Louis Hawks

1954-55: Bill Sharman,
Boston Celtics

1953-54: Bob Cousy,
Boston Celtics

1952-53: George Mikan,
Minneapolis Lakers

1951-52: Paul Arizin,
Philadelphia Warriors

1950-51: Ed Macauley,
Boston Celtics

NBA FINALS MVP WINNERS

2014-15: Andre Iguodala, Golden State Warriors

2013-14: Kawhi Leonard, San Antonio Spurs

2012-13: LeBron James, Miami Heat

2011-12: LeBron James, Miami Heat

2010-11: Dirk Nowitzki, Dallas Mavericks

2009-10: Kobe Bryant, Los Angeles Lakers

2008-09: Kobe Bryant, Los Angeles Lakers

2007-08: Paul Pierce, Boston Celtics

2006-07: Tony Parker, San Antonio Spurs

2005-06: Dwyane Wade, Miami Heat

2004-05: Tim Duncan, San Antonio Spurs

2003-04: Chauncey Billups, Detroit Pistons

2002-03: Tim Duncan, San Antonio Spurs

2001-02: Shaquille O'Neal, Los Angeles Lakers

2000-01: Shaquille O'Neal, Los Angeles Lakers

1999-00: Shaquille O'Neal, Los Angeles Lakers

1998-99: Tim Duncan, San Antonio Spurs

1997-98: Michael Jordan, Chicago Bulls

1996-97: Michael Jordan, Chicago Bulls

1995-96: Michael Jordan, Chicago Bulls

1994-95: Hakeem Olajuwon, Houston Rockets

1993-94: Hakeem Olajuwon, Houston Rockets

1992-93: Michael Jordan, Chicago Bulls

1991-92: Michael Jordan, Chicago Bulls

1990-91: Michael Jordan, Chicago Bulls

1989-90: Isiah Thomas, Detroit Pistons

1988-89: Joe Dumars, Detriot Pistons

1987-88: James Worthy, Los Angeles Lakers

1986-87: Earvin Johnson, Los Angeles Lakers

1985-86: Larry Bird, Boston Celtics

1984-85: Kareem Abdul-Jabbar, Los Angeles Lakers

1983-84: Larry Bird, Boston Celtics

1982-83: Moses Malone, Philadelphia 76ers

1981-82: Earvin Johnson, Los Angeles Lakers

1980-81: Cedric Maxwell, Boston Celtics

1979-80: Earvin Johnson, Los Angeles Lakers

1978-79: Dennis Johnson, Seattle SuperSonics

1977-78: Wes Unseld, Washington Bullets

1976-77: Bill Walton, Portland Trail Blazers

1975-76: Jo Jo White, Boston Celtics

1974-75: Rick Barry, Golden State Warriors

1973-74: John Havlicek, Boston Celtics

1972-73: Willis Reed, New York Knicks

1971-72: Wilt Chamberlain, Los Angeles Lakers

1970-71: Kareem Abdul-Jabbar, Milwaukee Bucks

1969-70: Willis Reed, New York Knicks

1968-69: Jerry West, Los Angeles Lakers

TIM DUNCAN

HAIRSTON
19

ACKNOWLEDGMENTS

FIRST, I'D LIKE to thank my editor, Steve Cameron, whose sharp eye for detail and ability to come up with multiple ways of saying rebounds and assists are exceptional qualities. His patience, guidance and steady hand are all over this book. I'd like to express my gratitude to publisher Lionel Koffler and all the staff at Firefly Books, as well as copyeditor Patricia MacDonald and designer Matt Filion, for their help in molding and shaping *Basketball Now!*—books are very much a collaboration, and the hard work of everyone involved is much appreciated.

Personally, I'd like to thank my parents, David and Esther-Jo, and my sister, Michelle, whose support has always been unwavering. While many friends and former colleagues have inspired me while writing this book, I'd like to particularly thank Jonathan and Andy, who watched a multitude of games with me this past season, especially our hometown Raptors, and who smiled patiently as I babbled on about my man crush for Steph Curry or the Raptors' inability to defend the pick and roll. I'd like to give a special shout-out to two of my oldest friends, Josh and Micah, for all those games of horse and twenty-one in my alleyway when we were kids growing up in Vancouver (RIP Grizzlies) and who form the nucleus of my earliest basketball memories beyond the Bulls' first three-peat and the drafting of Bryant "Big Country" Reeves. I can think of nothing better than spending a lazy summer afternoon shooting hoops, and it was during those formative years that I learned what it means to love sport. Finally, I'd like you thank you, the basketball fan, for reading!

– Adam Elliott Segal

No doubt this play was the result of the Raptors' inability to defend the pick and roll of the Bulls.

PROFILE INDEX

PHOTO CREDITS

ICON SPORTSWIRE
Albert Pena 144
Andrew Snook 86
Atlanta Journal-Constitution/Zuma Press 57
Bahram Mark Sobhani/Zuma Press 44-45
Carlos Gonzalez/Zuma Press 106-107, 124
Charles Fox/Zuma Press 116, 122
Chicago Tribune/Zuma Press 134-135, 148
Chris Sweda/Zuma Press 9, 30, 51, 158
Curtis Compton/Zuma Press 92, 94, 95
David Blair/Zuma Press 12, 32, 35, 55, 56, 64, 76-77, 78, 79, 84, 90, 91, 108, 110, 121
David T. Foster/Zuma Press 19, 53, 96, 143, 157
David Santiago/Zuma Press 49
Ed Crisostomo/Zuma Press 5, 24
Ed Suba Jr/Zuma Press 26, 118
El Nuevo Herald/Zuma Press 137
Hector Acevedo/Zuma Press 14
Hector Amezcua/Zuma Press 10-11
Hector Gabino/Zuma Press 48, 50, 123
Icon Sportswire 29, 58, 59, 65, 66, 88, 97, 111
Imago/Zuma Press 18, 62
Kevin Sullivan/Zuma Press 22, 23, 28, 105
Kevin Reece 155
Kyusung Gong/Zuma Press 15
Javier Rojas/Zuma Press 13
Jeff Siner/Zuma Press 142
Jeff Wheeler/Zuma Press 112, 125
Jim Cowsert/Zuma Press 145
Jose Luis Villegas/Zuma Press 82
Mark Alberti 20, 21
Mark Goldman 34, 54, 85, 141, 146, 147
Mark Hoffman/Zuma Press 46
MCT/Zuma Press 140
Miami Herald/Zuma Press 33
Nikki Boertman/Zuma Press 138, 150, 151
Nuccio Dinuzzo/Zuma Press 6, 31, 149
Oakland Tribune/Zuma Press 16
Orlando Sentinel/Zuma Press 120
Paul Rodriguez/Zuma Press 27
Pedro Portal/Zuma Press 136
Phil Masturzo/Zuma Press 89, 93
Prensa Internacional/Zuma Press 109
QMI Agency/Zuma Press 87
Ray Chavez/Zuma Press 2-3, 63
Richard W. Rodriguez/Zuma Press 61
Richard Ulreich/Zuma Press 113
Ronald Martinez/Pool/Zuma Press 25
Sacramento Bee/Zuma Press 83
Stephen Lew 47, 52

Steven M. Falk/Zuma Press 117
Susan Tripp Pollard/Zuma Press 60
The Commercial Appeal/Zuma Press 17, 80, 81, 139
TMB 119
Zuma Press 67

Cover:
Albert Pena (Anthony)
Al Diaz/Zuma Press (Wade)
Hector Acevedo/Zuma Press (James)
Icon Sportswire (Curry)
Kevin Sullivan/Zuma Press (Griffin)
Mark Halmas (Durant)

Back Cover:
David Blair/Zuma Press (Westbrook)
Chicago Tribune/Zuma Press (Noah)
Ed Crisostomo/Zuma Press (Harden)
The Commercial Appeal/Zuma Press (Gasol)

AP PHOTO
Associated Press 38, 153
Bettmann/Corbis 129
Bill Kostroun 101
David J. Phillip 114
Diane Bondareff 41
Elise Amendola 43
Eric Risberg 133
George Widman 40
Gerald Herbert 103
Greg Whal-Stephens 98, 100
Harold P. Matosian 131
Lynne Sladky 127
Mark J. Terrill 104
Marty Lederhandler 36
Matt Slocum 115
Mike Stone 130
Peter Southwick 102
Scott Troyanos 128
Susan Sterner 39
Tim Johnson 132

GETTY IMAGES
Carl Iwasaki 71
Jesse D. Garrabrant 75
Nathaniel S. Butler 68, 70
NBA Photos 73
Walter Iooss Jr. 72

Leabharlanna Poibli Chatha... ...tha Cliath
Dublin City Public Libraries